mgmt 350 #3

Learning to Lead

An Action Plan for Success

Revised Edition

Pat Heim, Ph.D., Elwood N. Chapman, and Serge Lashutka, M.B.A. and M.A.

A Crisp Fifty-Minute™ Series Book

This Fifty-Minute™ book is designed to be "read with a pencil." It is an excellent workbook for self-study as well as classroom learning. All material is copyright-protected and cannot be duplicated without permission from the publisher. *Therefore, be sure to order a copy for every training participant by contacting:*

THOMSON
NETg

1-800-442-7477 • 25 Thomson Place, Boston MA • www.courseilt.com

Learning to Lead

An Action Plan for Success

Revised Edition

Pat Heim, Ph.D., Elwood N. Chapman, and Serge Lashutka, M.B.A. and M.A.

CREDITS:

Product Manager: **Debbie Woodbury**
Editor: **Ann Gosch**
Production Editor: **Genevieve McDermott**
Production Artists: **Nicole Phillips, Rich Lehl, and Betty Hopkins**
Manufacturing: **Stephanie Porreca**

Trademarks
Crisp Fifty-Minute Series is a trademark of NETg. Some of the product names and company names used in this book have been used for identification purposes only, and may be trademarks or registered trademarks of their respective manufacturers and sellers.

Disclaimer
NETg reserves the right to revise this publication and make changes from time to time in its content without notice.

ISBN 10: 1-56052-683-1
ISBN 13: 978-1-56052-683-4
Library of Congress Catalog Card Number 2003106960
Printed in the United States of America
4 5 6 7 08 07 06

Learning Objectives For:

LEARNING TO LEAD

The objectives for *Learning to Lead, Revised Edition* are listed below. They have been developed to guide the user to the core issues covered in this book.

THE OBJECTIVES OF THIS BOOK ARE TO HELP THE USER:

1) Explore the qualities that make good leaders

2) Understand the role of leadership power in getting work done through others

3) Learn the importance of developing a vision and following it through

4) Obtain tools for managing change effectively

5) Learn strategies for leading people to work together effectively as a team

ASSESSING PROGRESS

NETg has developed a Crisp Series **assessment** that covers the fundamental information presented in this book. A 25-item, multiple-choice and true/false questionnaire allows the reader to evaluate his or her comprehension of the subject matter. To download the assessment and answer key, go to www.courseilt.com and search on the book title, or call 1-800-442-7477.

Assessments should not be used in any employee selection process.

About the Authors

Elwood N. Chapman's self-help books have sold more than two million copies. He is well known for his best-selling *Attitude, Your Most Priceless Possession; The New Supervisor; Comfort Zones;* and *Plan B: Converting Change into Career Opportunity.*

After a career as a successful college teacher, he retired in 1977 from his positions as professor of business at Chaffey College and visiting lecturer at Claremont Graduate School. "Chap," as his friends knew him, touched the lives of many through his teaching and writing.

Elwood Chapman died October 7, 1995, and—though his typewriter is silent—he continues to speak to us through the books that are his legacy. Those of us who knew him miss his cheerful smile, twinkling eyes, and wonderful attitude.

Pat Heim is CEO of The Heim Group, which provides management and organization development services, specializing in gender differences in the workplace, since 1983. Clients include Procter & Gamble, General Electric, and British Petroleum. Her other books include *Hardball for Women,* which the *Library Journal* called a landmark publication, and *In the Company of Women: Transforming Workplace Conflicts into Powerful Alliances.*

Serge Lashutka is senior consultant with The Heim Group. He provides organization development services to clients specializing in strategy, organization, and change issues. His clients include educational institutions and healthcare, entertainment, and high-tech companies. Serge designs and conducts workshops and learning experiences, and coaches executives, teams, and organizations through complex transitions, including reorganizations, acquisitions, and major shifts in technology and knowledge. Pat and Serge can be contacted at HeimGroup@aol.com.

How to Use This Book

This *Fifty-Minute™ Series Book* is a unique, user-friendly product. As you read through the material, you will quickly experience the interactive nature of the book. There are numerous exercises, real-world case studies, and examples that invite your opinion, as well as checklists, tips, and concise summaries that reinforce your understanding of the concepts presented.

A Crisp Learning *Fifty-Minute™ Book* can be used in a variety of ways. Individual self-study is one of the most common. However, many organizations use *Fifty-Minute* books for pre-study before a classroom training session. Other organizations use the books as a part of a systemwide learning program—supported by video and other media based on the content in the books. Still others work with Crisp Learning to customize the material to meet their specific needs and reflect their culture. Regardless of how it is used, we hope you will join the more than 20 million satisfied learners worldwide who have completed a *Fifty-Minute Book.*

Contents

Part 1: Exploring Your Leadership Potential

Part 2: Being Your Personal Best

Part 3: Being a Visionary

Part 4: Being a Change Agent

Part 5: Being a Team Leader

Part 6: Creating an Action Plan

Appendix

P A R T 1

Exploring Your
Leadership Potential

2

Differentiating Leaders from Managers

The differences between managers and leaders can be difficult to explain. Recognizing this, the following statements may help you distinguish the dimensions of leadership. Please review the statements to understand the differences between managers and leaders.

Managers vs. Leaders

A good Manager is content to follow directions and suggestions from above. A Leader is more likely to strive to understand the big picture of the organization and what needs to change in the future.

A good Manager is willing to accept responsibility. A Leader seeks new and increased responsibility.

An effective Manager will communicate with employees as necessary. A Leader realizes the importance of continual communication about the vision and how each employee contributes to that vision.

A Manager tends to accept the current team dynamics as a given. A Leader continuously works to improve team communication and cohesion.

A Manager is personally more apt to accept comfortable assignments. A Leader looks for more demanding opportunities to develop his or her leadership potential.

A good Manager usually accepts good performance that meets standards. A Leader is continually striving to help others to improve their performance.

Many Managers are content to set modest goals, try for a comfortable working environment, and improve efficiency. A Leader tends to set more demanding goals that challenge others and create a more dynamic working environment.

Managers see change as problems to be solved. Leaders see change as a natural and critical part of improved performance.

Is the distinction between managing and leading becoming clearer to you? The ideas and concepts in this book are presented so you can begin assessing your current skills and incorporating development activities to help you become a solid leader.

LEADERSHIP POTENTIAL SCALE

If you expect to become a manager or you already occupy a management position, you may wonder whether you have the potential to lead others. This exercise is designed to help you formulate an answer. Read the statement at both ends of the scale and then circle the number that best indicates where you fit. Most people fall somewhere between the two extremes.

	High **Low**	
I can be both an excellent manager and have time to lead.	10 9 8 7 6 5 4 3 2 1	I am satisfied being a good manager.
I am a visionary. I love to the plan for long-term goals.	10 9 8 7 6 5 4 3 2 1	I prefer to focus on day-to-day details.
I enjoy working with people and teams.	10 9 8 7 6 5 4 3 2 1	I would rather work alone.
I am willing to deal with others' performance problems.	10 9 8 7 6 5 4 3 2 1	I avoid dealing with others about performance problems.
I enjoy communication and have the potential to become outstanding.	10 9 8 7 6 5 4 3 2 1	My communication skills are adequate.
I have the desire to become a top leader.	10 9 8 7 6 5 4 3 2 1	I am comfortable as a follower.
I view change as a normal part of life.	10 9 8 7 6 5 4 3 2 1	I generally avoid change.
I enjoy rallying others around common goals.	10 9 8 7 6 5 4 3 2 1	I prefer others to provide direction for me.
I am willing to deal with and value conflict that arises on my team.	10 9 8 7 6 5 4 3 2 1	I do not like to handle conflict.
I enjoy developing people and seeing them grow.	10 9 8 7 6 5 4 3 2 1	I would rather focus on my own development and growth.

TOTAL _____

If you scored 80 or above, it would appear that you have a high desire and potential to be a leader. A rating between 60 and 80 shows good potential. A rating under 60 is a signal you may want to delay incorporating leadership practices into your management style.

Assessing Your Readiness for Leadership

Leadership at any level is built on basic management skills. Until an operation is well managed, the person in charge is not sufficiently free to lead. Thus, those attempting to lead without fundamental management competencies usually fail before they get started.

"You can't lead an organization if you are constantly putting out management-related fires."

"Some weeks it is all I can do to act as a caretaker around here. Lead? You've got to be kidding."

"I feel apologetic about the fact that I can free myself to lead only now and then."

First-level managers who desire to lead must learn to manage efficiently in such a way that they have the freedom to add the leadership dimension to their personal tool chest. This means that managers who want to lead must free themselves by learning to be:

➤ Outstanding at setting priorities, establishing goals, and managing their time

➤ Superior teachers, counselors, and delegators

➤ Excellent at developing and managing processes, systems, and controls

What are the dangers of reaching into leadership behaviors before excellent management practices are in position?

➤ You may be overwhelmed and perform your management job poorly

➤ Employees can feel confused and lose respect for the way you operate

➤ You may fail as a leader, which may leave you demoralized

First things first. Hone your management skills before jumping into leadership situations. In the next pages you will assess your management skills to determine if you are ready to take the leap into leadership.

PERSONAL MANAGEMENT ASSESSMENT SCALE

The following survey describes 20 practices common to excellent managers. While reading this book, keep clear in your mind the differences between a successful manager and a leader.

Please read all statements carefully. Then decide as a current manager how well you are performing these practices. Indicate your decision by circling the appropriate number.

	Current Level of Practice				
	Excellent	Very Good	Good	Modest	Poor
1. Strive to keep employees fully informed	5	4	3	2	1
2. Express my thoughts clearly	5	4	3	2	1
3. Am a good listener	5	4	3	2	1
4. Show compassion	5	4	3	2	1
5. Provide important rewards to staff	5	4	3	2	1
6. Win by allowing employees to also win	5	4	3	2	1
7. Have full backing from those under me	5	4	3	2	1
8. Am able to adapt to changes	5	4	3	2	1
9. Establish consistent, clear standards	5	4	3	2	1
10. Get tough when necessary	5	4	3	2	1
11. Am respected by employees when I use authority	5	4	3	2	1
12. Manage resources effectively	5	4	3	2	1
13. Consult with others in making decisions	5	4	3	2	1
14. Follow logical steps in making decisions	5	4	3	2	1

CONTINUED

	Current Level of Practice				
	Excellent	Very Good	Good	Modest	Poor
15. Admit my mistakes	5	4	3	2	1
16. Maintain a positive, upbeat attitude	5	4	3	2	1
17. Make work enjoyable	5	4	3	2	1
18. Implement personnel practices consistently	5	4	3	2	1
19. Delegate effectively	5	4	3	2	1
20. Am highly ethical in all situations	5	4	3	2	1

Total Score _____

Developing Your Personal Management Practices

Having a solid management foundation is critical for all successful leaders. If your score on the Personal Management Assessment Scale ranges from 80 to 100, you have your management practices on a good foundation. You are ready to develop your leadership skills.

If your score is between 60 and 80, you have some work to do in bolstering your management practices as you develop your leadership skills. If your score is less than 60, you must focus on further developing your management practices if you are going to be a successful leader.

Good leaders are always developing themselves further. Go back and review where you gave yourself the lowest scores and list below the three practices that are most important for you to develop. Below each practice, list the two or three actions you will take to further develop that management practice.

Management Practice 1: _____

    Action: _____

    Action: _____

    Action: _____

Management Practice 2: _____

    Action: _____

    Action: _____

    Action: _____

Management Practice 3: _____

    Action: _____

    Action: _____

    Action: _____

In Part 6 you will be invited to rank your management characteristics again, along with 20 leadership practices. This process will help you differentiate between management and leadership skills. It will also provide insight into the future role you desire for yourself and your personal development agenda. Remember, leaders never finish learning how to become more effective in achieving results through others.

MAKING A LEADERSHIP COMMITMENT

Not everyone aspires to lead. Some capable, valuable individuals are content to be excellent managers. These people prefer the recognition that comes from good management techniques. They leave visionary risks to others. At a certain point in their careers they would rather "follow" as a manager than lead others from a more demanding position. What about you?

Listed below are five major reasons that most managers elect to improve their leadership potential. Read each statement and check (✔) the square that most accurately reflects your feelings.

1. I seek more personal fulfillment than I can achieve in a management role. I want to feel I have improved the destiny of my organization.

   ❏ Exactly how I feel   ❏ Somewhat the way I feel   ❏ Not the way I feel

2. As a manager, I feel "boxed in." I want freedom to make more decisions and more power to execute them. Taking more responsibility will allow me to have more impact on the organization's future, and therefore my own.

   ❏ Exactly how I feel   ❏ Somewhat the way I feel   ❏ Not the way I feel

3. I want upward mobility. I want to climb the executive ladder higher and faster. It is important for me to achieve some really meaningful long-term goals.

   ❏ Exactly how I feel   ❏ Somewhat the way I feel   ❏ Not the way I feel

4. I have a desire to constantly learn and grow. I want to share my learning and also develop others to realize their potential.

   ❏ Exactly how I feel   ❏ Somewhat the way I feel   ❏ Not the way I feel

5. I am willing to invest in the long-term development of my team and organization.

   ❏ Exactly how I feel   ❏ Somewhat the way I feel   ❏ Not the way I feel

If you checked all items as "Exactly how I feel," you are committed to taking on the leadership challenge! If not, you may want to reassess your willingness to become a leader.

Being Your
Personal Best

12

Rethinking Leadership Traits

Not too long ago, psychologists and management experts believed it took a special combination of personality traits, or distinguishing characteristics, to become a successful leader. No one, however, was able to prove what many people started to call the Trait Theory.

Indeed, leaders that have been most successful and have taken their organizations to unprecedented levels of high performance may not be what you might have imagined. They often are not particularly charismatic and may even be introverted. In fact, they often display humility and modesty. And yet they are not wimps. They are driven to produce outstanding results and will do whatever it takes to get there.

These leaders are ambitious for the success of the company rather than for themselves. They want to position the organization for success so it can become even greater. Successful leaders also understand they cannot do this on their own. They build strong teams where honesty and support of others are highly valued.

Leadership Traits Today

Today experts agree that there is no single set of traits or behaviors that will guarantee a person's success in leadership. But most experts suggest that the following behaviors are critical. Successful leaders tend to be:

➤ Hard on the important issues that hold back superior performance, but not hard on the people

➤ Self-deprecating—they don't take themselves too seriously

➤ Relentlessly pursuing new ways of achieving higher performance through others

➤ Aware of both the personal and professional lives of their employees

➤ Ready to rise to the challenge when they hear that an important goal "cannot be done"

➤ Always looking to ensure there are clear group goals that engage the excitement and commitment of others

➤ Concerned about developing trust and group cohesiveness while also valuing differences and conflict

➤ Consistent in communicating a set of messages about future direction and helping people see continuity during times of rapid change

➤ Willing to learn and change without being defensive, which allows others to approach them openly with new information and specific feedback

Understanding and Using Leadership Power

All leaders must have and use power effectively to be successful. After all, power is the ability to get things done through others. Without leadership power, employees would not be inspired to reach for new and challenging goals. Leaders must use their power to influence others and help them through change. This influence affects how people think and feel, what they believe, and what they do.

Yet we have all seen leaders who have wielded their power in ways that have resulted in employees being frustrated, confused, and even angry. You also may have seen leaders who failed to use their power when the situation called for strong leadership.

Striking the right balance results in employees who are energized, excited, and eager to get on to the next challenge. You must understand the nuances of power so you can develop positive results in using your power and minimize the potentially negative outcomes.

Your goal in seeking power must not be about your personal ends, but what it can do to help you and your team have a positive impact on your organization.

Three Sources of Leadership Power

To be a successful leader, you must understand where power comes from and how best to develop it. There are three sources of power for becoming an effective leader:

> ➤ **Role power**

> ➤ **Relationship power**

> ➤ **Knowledge power**

Too often leaders overuse one source of power, preventing them from being as effective as they might. Being flexible in the type of power to draw on allows you to be successful in a wider range of circumstances.

The following sections explain how to develop each of the three sources of leadership power, when to use power and when not to use it, and how to develop a reserve of power in case you need it unexpectedly. You also will learn how developing the power of others will enhance your own power as a leader.

Wielding Role Power Judiciously

Just by being the manager, you have some authority over others. This authority is your *role power*—the power you have simply because of your position. Outstanding leaders know how to strike the right balance among the three components of role power:

➤ *"Do it because I am the boss."*

   Yes, you are the designated "boss," so you lead the team. But be careful in using this approach too frequently because it diminishes employee motivation and involvement.

➤ *"We need to talk."*

   If you have an employee who is not performing, you may need to engage in performance management and the disciplinary process. Before you do, ensure the employee knows how to do the task, has the resources, and does not have any barriers that are preventing him or her from doing the task.

➤ *"Great job!"*

   When an employee or team has done an outstanding job, you have the ability to provide rewards because of your position as leader. Try to catch employees doing things right, or close to right, and give them public praise so people know what good performance looks like.

Avoiding the Pitfalls of Role Power

Outstanding leaders know that the most effective options in achieving high performance in leading others are performance management ("We need to talk") and rewards ("Great job!"). But depending on role power too much can cause a backlash. Employees will do what you in your role have asked and expect of them, rather than what they judge to be the right action.

Using role power exclusively can cause employees to mentally check out and do only what the boss says. Employee contributions and ideas tend to dry up, and employees may even become resentful when their ideas are not solicited.

Moreover, if you are a new manager, relying on role power alone is especially risky. You may not yet have established any power other than that consigned by your role, which means you must be humble enough to recognize that the power is in the role, not in you. The power would still be there no matter who occupied the role. With this in mind, see if you agree or disagree with the following statements by checking (✔) the appropriate square.

Agree	Disagree	
❏	❏	True leaders do not need to remind team members that they are in charge.
❏	❏	The best use of role power is to maintain discipline. Sometimes it must be used to focus a group on a key performance issue.
❏	❏	It is possible to communicate your role power through your actions and activities.
❏	❏	When people respect you as a person, they are more likely to respect the role you occupy.
❏	❏	When someone says, "the new supervisor's job has gone to his head," the speaker means that role power is being abused.
❏	❏	Leaders who seek more role power must learn how to use it in a sensitive manner at the very beginning.

If you agreed with all of these statements, you are comfortable with downplaying your role power and building up your relationship and knowledge power bases to motivate employees. Indeed, the more effectively you use the power in your relationships with your employees and in your knowledge of your company and the marketplace, the less you will need to use role power.

Defining Relationship Power

One of the most potent sources of power you have as a leader is your relationship with employees. When you have a positive relationship with an employee, you have a high "chip" value. Unfortunately, you can also lose chips, or "points," with employees, which leads to a negative relationship.

The important thing to keep in mind in managing your relationship power is that people always "make it equal." Some leaders think employees must do whatever they say. But what these leaders fail to understand is that employees will find some way, someday, to figure out how to make things equal in the end.

Jordan Mismanages His Chips

Jordan was hired from outside the company to manage a group of technicians. His employees traveled a great deal and not to the nicest of places.

The company had a "safe arrival call" policy. That is, when employees traveled on company business, they could call home upon arrival to inform their family they had arrived safely. There was an "official" dollar limit on these calls, but most of the employees were unaware of it.

Upon stepping into his job as manager, Jordan was investigating the files and found his employees had spent more on their calls than officially allowed, after which he proceeded to collect money from them: "Ted, you owe $3.12; Stacey, you owe $5.72; Brandon, $8.96."

The reaction was immediate. You could feel the electricity in the air. The team had a clear and common purpose: Get even with Jordan.

From then on, the wrong person would show up with the wrong equipment at the wrong site. This happened repeatedly. Jordan worked on stopping the never-ending errors. What Jordan did not understand is that people always make it equal in the end. The problem was not poor coordination of activities, but rather Jordan's massive chip deficit with his team.

This example illustrates the principle that every employee is an accountant. Realize that employees are keeping a chip account with you, and they know where you stand with them at any moment. You are gaining and losing chips all day, every day.

HELLO, MR. CHIPS

The best boss you ever had is probably someone who developed a large chip surplus with you. Name your best boss:_____

Check (✔) the box next to any of the statements below that were true of you when you worked with this leader.

I was willing to do something for my boss even if it:

- ❏ Was not part of my job
- ❏ Required me to work late
- ❏ Was not what I had planned on doing
- ❏ Required me to change my personal plans
- ❏ Was not something I liked to do
- ❏ Really was someone else's job
- ❏ Other_____

What did this leader do to build up a chip surplus?

_____

_____

_____

Managing Your "Chip" Account

To manage your relationship power effectively, it is important to build up and retain a chip surplus account with your employees. Then they will be there when you really need them.

The key to building a high chip value is discerning what chips your employees value. Different employees value different chips, as illustrated in the following example.

Different Strokes for Different Folks

Jennifer worked in a healthcare setting, and her administrative assistant, Isabel, had a windowless office. It did not take long for Jennifer to realize that Isabel highly valued interaction. Each time Jennifer walked into Isabel's windowless cubicle, she spent an extra minute or so talking to Isabel about what was happening around the office, noticing Isabel's new outfit, and asking about her children.

One day Jennifer was meeting with Dana, her colleague, when Isabel walked in with some work she had finished for Jennifer. After Isabel handed this work to Jennifer and left, Dana asked, "When did you give her that work?" Jennifer responded, "This morning, why?" With some irritation in her voice, Dana retorted, "I gave her work three days ago, and she never brings her finished work to me."

The problem was that Dana did not pay Isabel the interaction chips Isabel valued so much. And people always make it equal in the end.

Not too long after this, Jennifer changed jobs and began working with a group that was populated primarily with engineers. What Jennifer quickly learned was that if she spent the same amount of time interacting with the engineers, it cost her chips. The engineers, unlike Isabel, did not value interaction the same way. They preferred short and to-the-point task conversations. Switching to this concise behavior earned Jennifer chips with the engineers, who did not want to "waste" time on interpersonal conversation.

You as a leader must discern which chips your employees value. When you have determined what individuals value the most, then you can sincerely work toward building up a chip surplus account with them. You can draw on this surplus, but remember to keep replenishing the account.

Avoiding a Chip Deficit

A chip deficit occurs when the other person perceives he has given more chips than he has received. Avoid being in a chip deficit with employees because they may create negative consequences for you that you never imagined. These consequences could include:

➤ Neglecting to give you important messages

➤ Creating a schedule for you that is particularly arduous

➤ Missing deadlines

➤ "Forgetting" important assignments

➤ Not warning you about potential problems

➤ Doing *exactly* what you have said when they know you have misspoken

➤ Being unavailable to work overtime on the day of the big crunch

➤ Developing amnesia about where you are when your boss calls looking for you

Realizing the Power of Knowledge

Knowledge power has become more important as our society has become increasingly technical and roles have become more specialized. Knowledge power includes a broad view of the company, its strengths, the competition, customers wants, and the challenges of the marketplace.

Just having this knowledge is not enough and does not make you powerful. It is in the sharing and use of this knowledge with others that knowledge power is exercised. This means influencing the thinking and actions of others through what you know and are learning.

Many managers and leaders foolishly downplay knowledge as a power source. But knowledge power may be the safest and best way to demonstrate leadership. Reflect for a moment on why most people respect mentors. Isn't it because the mentor provides knowledge and guidance? If you agree, then you should strive to be both a mentor and a leader to your staff—in other words, be an outstanding teacher. Share your knowledge.

Knowledge Power Profile

I could make a 15-minute presentation to my work group on the following topics:

	Agree				Disagree
Our competitors	1	2	3	4	5
Our industry	1	2	3	4	5
Company strategy	1	2	3	4	5
Key company goals	1	2	3	4	5
Key company processes	1	2	3	4	5
Key company initiatives	1	2	3	4	5
Financial results and reports	1	2	3	4	5
My key technical expertise	1	2	3	4	5
Teamwork	1	2	3	4	5
Leadership	1	2	3	4	5
Change management	1	2	3	4	5
Communication	1	2	3	4	5
Group goals	1	2	3	4	5
Management	1	2	3	4	5

Other areas:

_____	1	2	3	4	5
_____	1	2	3	4	5
_____	1	2	3	4	5

Learning and Leading

If you move up in an organization, inevitably you will have people reporting to you whose specific knowledge and expertise will exceed your own. But do not worry if you do not know how to do the job of everyone who reports to you. Knowledge power involves not only sharing your knowledge with your employees so they can develop, but also learning along with them. This is not about being a know-it-all, but about learning so you can use your knowledge in the service and development of others.

Acquiring knowledge never ends because things keep changing. Your unique leadership contribution is knowing when and how to pull the right people together who do hold the necessary knowledge and information to tackle an important problem or to address a valuable new opportunity.

With this in mind, please mark whether you agree or disagree with the following statements about knowledge power by checking (✔) the appropriate square.

Agree	Disagree	
❏	❏	Leaders need to be more sensitive to and generous in sharing their knowledge.
❏	❏	Of the three sources, knowledge power is the best way to earn respect from an employee.
❏	❏	The more you know about your job or business, the more knowledge power you have. Translated, this means the best use of knowledge power is to continue to learn.
❏	❏	It is possible to overuse knowledge power and wind up being viewed as a know-it-all.
❏	❏	One of the best ways to empower employees is to share your knowledge.
❏	❏	Leaders need not be as sensitive in the use of knowledge power as of role power.
❏	❏	Most managers and leaders have more knowledge power than they realize, so they tend to underuse it.
❏	❏	Practical experience is an excellent way to gain more knowledge power.

If you agree with these statements, you see the value of knowledge power as a leader.

For more information, read *Excellence in Management* by Rick Conlow, Thomson Learning.

Communicating Confidence Through Non-Verbal Cues

Employees want a leader who is confident and self-assured. This provides them with a sense of stability and direction. Following people who do not seem assured of where they are going can be scary.

One of the primary ways we communicate our confidence is through non-verbal cues. If you want to lead others, you must look as though you know where you are going. The following are some of the ways we communicate this non-verbally:

➢ **Dress**

How you dress communicates a great deal about where you fit into the organization. Take your cue for work attire from the leaders upstairs. (Special note for women: Although casual attire has become common in many organizations, female managers who wear casual attire often are not perceived as managers.)

➢ **Physical Presence**

Individuals who are naturally more confident tend to take up more physical space. When it is important for you to appear powerful, as when giving a presentation, counseling an employee, or participating in a significant meeting, notice how you hold your body. Do you pull in and get small, which subconsciously communicates powerlessness, or do push up and spread out, which communicates confidence?

➢ **Demeanor**

Realize you are being watched all the time. People are making assessments about what is going on with you, the department, and the organization from your whole demeanor. It is surprising how often people wonder if a company is in trouble simply because of how the managers appear in the corridors. Head down, hands in pockets, and slumped shoulders can send unintentional signals to the workforce.

➢ **Facial Expressions**

One of the most powerful expressions is the stone face. Be careful not to smile when the situation does not call for it.

> **Gestures**

When we are in uncomfortable situations, we tend to use telltale gestures. Next time you are stuck in a traffic jam, look at the drivers around you. You will see people rubbing their necks, scratching their noses, and running their fingers through their hair. These are called comfort cues. Make sure you refrain from these gestures that communicate your lack of confidence.

> **Voice**

When we are unsure of ourselves, we often communicate this insecurity through our voice. For example, when challenged in a meeting at which we are not confident, our voice may shake and become higher pitched or softer. Be sure to notice and manage the quality of your voice when you are under stress.

FAKE IT UNTIL YOU MAKE IT

New leaders sometimes are unsure of how to develop the confidence they need in their role. One way is to observe other leaders in various situations and understand how they communicate confidence, particularly through their non-verbal behavior.

Select situations you have observed where you felt the leaders expressed confidence. Describe the leaders' behavior in the spaces that follow. By making careful observations, you can pick up important ideas on how to improve the confidence you are communicating.

	Situation 1	Situation 2	Situation 3
A. Dress	_____	_____	_____
B. Physical Presence	_____	_____	_____
C. Demeanor	_____	_____	_____
D. Facial Expressions	_____	_____	_____
E. Gestures	_____	_____	_____
F. Voice	_____	_____	_____

Consider the behaviors of these confident leaders. Sometimes we must behave *as if* we are confident to begin feeling confident as a new leader. Going into your next meeting with a poised demeanor can start you on the path of developing the necessary confidence you need.

What could you incorporate as a new behavior that would best improve the perception of your confidence?

_____

_____

Projecting a Leadership Attitude

Few would disagree that attitude is a significant and powerful characteristic in every leader's repertoire. A positive attitude is necessary to project a winning leadership image—charismatic or not. A positive attitude is recognized as the "magic" that transmits the best of anyone's personality. A negative attitude closes the door.

Attitude is simply the way you view the world around you. It is a perceptual or mental phenomenon. It is your focus on life. In a sense, you see what you want to see. If you concentrate on negative factors (and there are plenty), eventually you will wind up with a negative attitude. When you concentrate on positive factors, you are more apt to stay positive. It sounds easy when you say "look at the bright side," but of course it is not. A positive attitude can be everyone's most priceless possession. To a leader it is essential.

Attitude also is the way you look at yourself. If you see yourself as a successful leader, then success is more likely to occur. Consider these statements about leadership attitudes:

➤ When you are positive, all those around you are positively influenced

➤ A positive attitude converts a personality that is easy to ignore into one that is not

➤ A leader with a negative attitude does not keep followers for long

➤ People reach their personality potential when they have a positive attitude

➤ Individuals are more creative when they are positive

➤ A positive attitude releases the enthusiasm stored up inside individuals, which gives them more confidence to play out their roles as leaders

---

For more information, read *Attitude: Your Most Priceless Possession* by Elwood N. Chapman and Wil McKnight, Thomson Learning.

CASE STUDY: SELECTING THE BEST AVAILABLE MODEL

Crystal devoted the first several months following her promotion to becoming an excellent manager. She read extensively and took all available seminars on management-related topics. She applied techniques and principles alike. Her superiors were more than pleased with her performance.

During this period Crystal fashioned her behavior around a manager who turned out to be a mentor. Then it occurred to her that the managers in her mentor's department were not promoted into leadership roles. Why was that? After talking with others and thinking it through, Crystal decided that her "model" had not demonstrated enough leadership. He was a solid manager, but tended to focus on today's needs, was slow to implement changes, and had strong employees who did not act as a team.

As a result, Crystal switched models. She discovered Corinne, who was both a strong leader and manager. Crystal began thinking about the company's long-term future and how her department could contribute to it. She also began to think about the necessary changes for the future and how best to implement these changes.

Crystal also recognized another manager, Kevin, who had built a strong team. She began talking to him about how to build an effective team. Daily she became more conscious of her sources of power and how to use them more effectively. In talking it over with her husband, Crystal said, "I just decided that I had to start acting like a leader if I wanted upward mobility."

Is this typical of a situation in your organization? Are excellent managers often left in their roles? Is it necessary to become a leader/manager to gain upward mobility? Defend your position in the space that follows.

_____

_____

Compare your answers with the authors' suggestions in the Appendix.

Summary of Part 2

Naturally, the more personal power you develop, the stronger you can be in your role as a leader. You will be able to communicate more effectively. You will be more convincing when you ask others to accept your vision. Your chip balance will help you lead through difficult situations.

But it is not always how much power you have. More important is how you employ it. Sensitivity to others is the key. And sensitivity is facilitated when knowledge power and role power are balanced with relationship power. Many variables are involved.

Part 2 presents the following points for balancing your power sources:

❏ You have three sources of power for becoming an effective leader—role, relationship, and knowledge.

❏ Role power can help you become an effective manager, but it is not your most effective source of power to becoming a leader.

❏ Do not underestimate the impact of relationship power. Individuals who are motivated by how you have personally affected their lives are willing to go the extra mile when the going gets tough.

❏ Use and share your knowledge power with others. Unleashing the knowledge power of others makes for better outcomes and improved performance.

❏ Becoming effective in developing your knowledge power and relationship power is a lifelong journey. Each day find one way to further improve your use of power.

PART 3

Being a Visionary

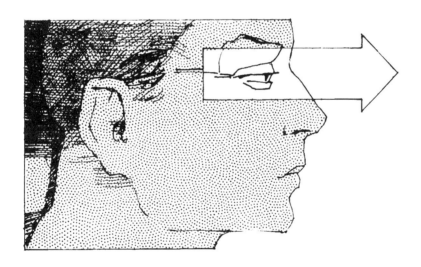

32

Knowing Where You Are Going

Good managers run a tight ship in their department. They stay within their budget and ensure that employees are productive and deadlines arc met. But think of the leaders you admire and you will usually find that they inspire people to do more than just "mind the store." Status quo is not enough: Leaders are on the move, improving, growing, and expanding into new areas. Visionary leaders focus on the big picture and longer-term future.

What further distinguishes leaders is that their growth has a direction. They know where they are going; they have a vision to which they are drawn. They are constantly aware of the challenges in their organization and are looking for opportunities to contribute. As an employee, you might be charting new territory with your leader. The process is exciting.

Taking Your Team with You

To be a true leader, you must have a sense of what is important and how you can contribute and make a mark. What do you value and how can you make those values contribute in a larger sense? If your ultimate aims are based on self-interest, employees are not going to be highly motivated to go the extra mile. On the other hand, if your team can see how your direction can make a difference to the company's performance and what they value, their energy and focus will support your goals.

At times managers will say, "There is no way I can shape my department. That's done by those above me." In the end, however, you have a choice either to create your future or let others do it for you. Recall the leaders you admire. They did not accept the status quo. Chances are they pushed, nudged, and changed the way things were previously done.

When leaders run into problems with other departments, they engage in developing win-win solutions rather than seeing these problems as win-lose. This is not about being right or wrong, but achieving better performance for the whole organization.

Once you begin to get a picture of your larger goal or vision, you can begin to strategize. The focus is more on the "how" rather than the "what." A word of caution: In the past decade or two, we have glorified quantitative decision-making. This has led some to focus a disproportional amount of attention on the correct calculations.

But your vision cannot be determined with a calculator or a case study. It must be what matters most to you. There are no rights or wrongs when it comes to a vision—just what is passionately important to you. If you cannot feel passionate about your current job and organization, you may want to consider leaving to find a position where you can express your passion.

CASE STUDY: EXPANDING YOUR VISION

Donny was the manager of the heat-treatment process on an assembly line. He asked a visiting management consultant to help him get Fred off his back. Fred was the manager of the next step in the assembly process. Fred continually complained to Donny that when his employees assembled the heat-treated parts from Donny's group, the parts often broke. This resulted in a large number of parts being scrapped.

Donny's primary concern was how to get Fred to stop his complaining. From Donny's view, he was doing his job just the way it was supposed to be done. All the parts were heat treated to specifications.

The consultant asked Donny, "Is the heat treatment causing the parts to break in Fred's area?"

Donny paused and sheepishly replied, "Well, it could be, but I am treating all the parts just as specified. So it really isn't my problem."

If Donny were to take a leadership role in this problem, rather than his present management perspective, what would he do?

_____

_____

_____

_____

_____

Compare your answer to the authors' response in the Appendix.

WHERE IS YOUR TELESCOPE FOCUSED?

The following questions will help you take a broader view of your department and organization. Think about how you might achieve better performance for the whole organization and write your responses in the spaces provided.

What other departments does your function affect? Have you asked the managers in these functions what you can do to make their jobs easier or to improve the quality of your organization's products and services? If so, what responses have you received?

_____

_____

Which functions affect the quality in your own department's product and services? Have you spoken to the managers of these functions about what you might do to improve the quality of your product or service? If so, what responses have you received?

_____

_____

Do you know what your organization's biggest challenges are, and have you examined how you and your department can address these challenges? Explain.

_____

_____

Have you asked employees what might be changed so that they can more effectively do their jobs?

_____

_____

What new technologies or processes might improve the performance of your group?

_____

_____

Avoiding the Roadblocks in the Details

To lead a group, you must not lose sight of the long view. You need to see the patterns, trends, and opportunities rather than get caught up in the details, particularly when these immediate details loom as roadblocks. If you are true to your dream, your roadblocks will become mere hurdles to overcome.

Successful managers and leaders use these strategies for staying focused and overcoming the roadblocks that details can pose.

➤ **No Details Until 10 A.M.**

Many managers work best in the morning, yet they often find that this time is consumed by small issues. To stay focused on their larger goals, some managers set a rule that they are not to be interrupted and no meetings are to be scheduled until 10 A.M. During this time, they shut their door and get their serious work underway.

➤ **Your Top Six**

A top executive of a large international corporation sets her focus at the end of each day. Before she leaves work, she writes down the six most important activities for the next day. When she comes in the next morning, she handles these six items first before she gets pulled into daily details.

➤ **Assess Your Focus**

Think about yesterday. What percentage of your time was spent moving toward your vision and long-term goals and what percentage dealt with the daily drama of life? Balance is the key.

For more tips, read *Time Management* by Marion Haynes, Thomson Learning.

CASE STUDY: TOO MUCH ATTENTION TO DETAIL?

Barbara has always taken professional pride in her accounting skills. She was a top student in school and has excelled in her job. In recognition of her performance, Barbara was named accounting manager.

Barbara's attention to detail was always one of her greatest assets. Now that she is in management, the details of her position have increased tenfold and she feels as if she is drowning. Her greatest asset has become a liability.

To get a handle on things, Barbara has always made lists. But there are not enough hours to deal with everything on her lists. To make matters worse, her boss has begun to ask questions about her focus and where she is "taking her department."

Barbara is beginning to wonder if she is really cut out for leadership. What would you recommend she do?

_____

_____

_____

_____

_____

Compare your answer to the authors' response in the Appendix.

Making Decisions According to Your Vision

Always take the long view in decision-making, particularly for important decisions. As a leader, you must demonstrate focus and consistency. Underlying these qualities are your values and how you see yourself contributing to your department, organization, or industry. For example, regardless of responsibility, leaders want products and services with the most integrity, the highest quality, the safest reputation, the most dependability, and so on.

This value focus drives decisions. There is no compromise. As a leader you may need to sacrifice a short-term goal to stay true to your vision. Do it! Nothing is more important than the big picture.

Consistency in where you are leading your employees is extremely important. Employees find it hard to keep that extra level of motivation if decisions indicate they are headed one way today and another direction tomorrow. The consistency of your decisions signals your commitment to what you believe to be important.

The following is an excellent summary of a decision process outlined in *Successful Self-Management**.

> ➤ Make the best decision you can—*by doing it*—and then observe your results.

> ➤ Avoid "perfection paralysis." Not everything you do will be perfect, but if you start with a "rough draft" and then shape and improve things as you go, you will end up fine. Keep the big picture in mind.

> ➤ Use a decision guide like the one illustrated below.

1. Does it add value to our vision?
2. What will happen to our vision if I don't do it?
3. Can I delegate it?
4. Can I spend less time on it?"

Successful Self-Management by Paul Timm, Thomson Learning.

PUTTING YOUR VISION INTO ACTION

You may be clear on your vision, but it is often difficult for employees to see your vision's relationship to daily activities, understand their part in that vision, or even support the vision without working at cross-purposes with you. The key to turning ideas into reality is communication, both orally and in writing. Leaders are clear about the goals they set for themselves and for their followers.

The statements below will help you see where you stand on leadership skills related to your vision. Read the statement in both columns and then place a check (✔) in the appropriate square.

❑ I plan long term.	❑ I focus on getting through the day or week.
❑ I determine what direction my teams should take.	❑ I wait for direction from above.
❑ I focus on how my area of responsibility serves the organization and our customers.	❑ I focus on what my department is supposed to do.
❑ I share my vision with employees and help guide their work.	❑ Employees know what to do; they have their day-to-day assignments.
❑ I look at what is needed for my personal growth.	❑ I'm too busy to worry about personal growth and development.
❑ My employees are clear about how to be a success in their job.	❑ My employees are comfortable doing what they do.
❑ I consciously manage and shape change in my department.	❑ Changes occur and there is little I can do about them.
❑ I plan for the growth and development of my employees.	❑ We're too busy around here for personal growth and development.
❑ I encourage my employees to try new methods.	❑ I would rather my employees use the tried-and-true methods of doing their work.

═CONTINUED═

CONTINUED

- ☑ We celebrate personal and departmental successes.
- ☑ I provide my employees with information and articles about what is happening in our industry.

- ❏ We keep our noses to the grindstone.
- ❏ What my employees read and the information they have aren't my job.

If you checked more boxes in the left column, you are on your way to becoming a leader. It is time to put your vision into concrete steps. The next sections will explain how to do so.

Communicating Your Vision

Leaders generate excitement, interest, and energy in others through communication. How you talk about your vision will determine how much others will want to mentally "sign up" to follow you. Two keys to communicating effectively about your vision are consistency and repetition. Let's look at each of these in more detail.

Consistency

Leaders are usually eager to describe their vision and they do it in a predictable way. This is not because they lack creativity. It is because their vision does not change from day to day. What leaders focus on is how the future will look as a result of their vision. They describe the benefits inherent in their vision and their personal belief in its importance.

A vision is not a set speech given from notes at formal occasions. Instead, it is impromptu and delivered to anyone who will listen. If you want others to follow you, you have to get out and describe where you are going. The consistency becomes important so that others will get a clear picture of where you are taking them.

Sometimes managers find communicating a vision difficult. It is more comfortable to stay in the office and do a job. That is not leadership! Communicating your vision is not about being charismatic or bombastic. It is about weaving what you see as possible for the future into everyday conversations in the hallway, comments in staff meetings, and presentations in more formal settings. The idea is to get people excited about the future and to help them see specific contributions they can make to create a compelling future.

Repetition

Once is not enough. Initially people will wonder if you are serious or if this is just the "flavor of the month." That is why your communication must be continuous and repetitive. After people hear the message frequently enough and see that your behaviors are consistent with your message, then—and only then—will they begin to believe you are serious. When they know you are determined, they also will begin to believe in your vision. An added plus to repetition is focus. If you keep talking about your vision, then you will not lose sight of the target.

For more information, read *Organization, Vision, Values, and Mission* by Cynthia Scott, Dennis Jaffe, and Glenn Tobe, Thomson Learning.

Working with Stakeholders

Although it is fine to communicate your vision to anyone who will listen, you also must target selected individuals and groups—your stakeholders.

Stakeholders are those who can help or hinder you in attaining your vision because they have something at stake. Certainly this includes your employees and your manager. But others are also important, such as your peers, managers of other departments, senior management, peers outside the organization, or your family, to name just a few.

On the *help* side, stakeholders are people who can provide you with information, ideas, finances, a good word, or even emotional support. On the *hinder* side, they may be individuals who see your ideas as threatening to their power or security, or people who support the status quo.

To be strategic, you must know who these people are. Take a minute to jot down names or initials.

Likely to Help   **Likely to Hinder**

_____   _____

_____   _____

_____   _____

If some of your stakeholders are people you do not normally see in your day-to-day business, you may need to create opportunities to chat with them about your vision. You could try the following:

➤ Invite stakeholders to your department meeting

➤ Ask their advice about an idea or problem

➤ Take them to lunch

➤ Send them a book or article

➤ Invite them to serve on a committee

➤ Involve them in a planning session

Other opportunities you could try:

_____

_____

Creating Goals to Reach Your Vision

Your vision is your picture of the future. It is global and not precise. It is critical to have a vision, but a vision alone is not enough. You also must create specific goals to reach it. Think of your vision as where you would like to go. Think of your goals as the specifics about how to get there. It is important to write down both your vision and your goals. Goals have a limited time horizon. Some leaders write yearly goals; others prefer writing goals every six months. Choose whatever time horizon seems best for you.

To work, goals must have specific built-in components. Here is how to write goals that work:

➤ Be specific. Identify either the exact outcome you want or the process (how much by when).

➤ Make goals measurable. How will you measure whether you have been successful or not? Where is your goal line and how will you know if you have crossed it?

➤ Goals must be reasonable. Sometimes in our exuberance about an idea, we set goals that are impossible to reach and then we become discouraged. Make sure your goals are humanly possible given your present demands.

➤ Goals must be time specific—not "as soon as I can," but "by May 23."

An important aspect of goal setting is not to get bogged down in paperwork writing goals for everything. Be strategic. What are the most important targets you must hit to achieve your vision? Three to five goals may be appropriate and never more than eight. Some examples follow.

Sample Goals

"Institute a customer service survey by January 5. This survey will be mailed to all of our customers each quarter. The survey will inquire about: 1) quality of the product, 2) delivery time, and 3) assistance provided on the toll-free telephone number. Results from the survey will be compiled and presented at the quarterly planning meeting, and then a future target will be set."

"Increase our department's total sales volume this year over last year's by 17% by year's end. This goal assures maintaining the present level of customer satisfaction as measured by our Customer Satisfaction Report."

"Design an office layout for the new offices by October 15. The layout will include work stations for all employees and fulfillment space that allows for a 30% addition over the present area."

For more information, read *Goals and Goal Setting* by Larrie Rouillard, Thomson Learning.

START WRITING GOALS

Try writing your goals. What do you want to accomplish in the next year or sooner to move you toward your vision?

For each goal you list below, check (✔) whether it meets the goal-setting criteria of being specific, measurable, reasonable, and time specific.

Goal	Specific?	Measurable?	Reasonable?	Time Specific?
1)				
2)				
3)				
4)				
5)				

Note: Goals can never be set in concrete; organizations are too dynamic. This process is your best assessment at the time and will probably have to change to some degree during the year. Vision, on the other hand, is constant. How you go about achieving your vision may have to be altered as factors in the environment change.

Involve your employees in goal setting. Employees who are new to the organization and in training may find it difficult to contribute. Or they may find it enlightening.

CASE STUDY: PRESSURE FROM ABOVE

Miranda is the customer service manager in a large organization and her employees are about to revolt. Two weeks ago in her staff meeting, she told them that senior management was very concerned about the labor budget. Employees had to increase their number of calls. No excuses would be allowed. Productivity as measured by call numbers was the only goal.

Her employees took her to heart. They processed more customer calls than ever. But customer-complaint calls skyrocketed. Customers complained that they were not listened to, were cut off mid-sentence, and more. Now Miranda is telling her staff that customer service is more important than productivity.

This morning she announced to her staff that the quarterly report is due in a week—and that it is now top priority. Her employees do not know what is most important or where to focus their energy.

How would you counsel Miranda if you were her superior?

_____
_____
_____
_____
_____

Compare your answers to the authors' suggestions in the Appendix.

Summary of Part 3

Part 3 presents the following suggestions for becoming a visionary leader:

❑ Take the time to learn and develop a view of the big picture of your organization and industry and where they are going.

❑ Determine how your department can contribute to that future.

❑ Assess what other functions and departments could affect your area positively if changes were made.

❑ Consider what other areas your department could affect positively by changing how it works.

❑ Delegate the detail.

❑ Assess how consistently and how often you communicate your vision.

❑ Link up with the important stakeholders you have identified.

❑ Write down specific goals that will help you accomplish your vision.

P A R T 4

Being a

Change Agent

50

Leading People Through Change

In today's business world, it is said that change is the only constant. As a leader, you will need to see leading change as a big part of your role. Great leaders are able to help others transition through one change after another. Learning about change is a lifelong experience.

How ready are you to lead people through one change after another? Mark whether you agree or disagree with the following statements by checking (✔) the appropriate box.

Agree	Disagree	
❏	❏	Learning from mistakes can help your staff prepare for future successes.
❏	❏	People who "resist change" may have important information or views that need to be heard.
❏	❏	Leading change means telling people why change needs to happen, what is needed, and then involving them in figuring out how best to accomplish it.
❏	❏	Developing your own knowledge and understanding of the business challenges is important to successfully leading and communicating change.
❏	❏	Involving people in understanding the business issues and the major challenges and why key initiatives are being implemented can help prepare people to accept and respond to future changes.
❏	❏	People almost always need to see some benefit or payoff if they are going to change their behavior.
❏	❏	Your personal support and belief in a change is important to successfully leading a change.
❏	❏	Working with other leaders to understand where the business is going and what is needed from your group is an important part of leading change.
❏	❏	Providing opportunities to develop and learn new skills can help people become more positive and effective during future changes.

If you agreed with these comments, you are on your way to seeing change from a leadership perspective rather than as a manager.

Assessing Potential Organizational Change

Leaders are constantly looking for ways to improve performance and are asking people to change. Whether it is improving customer service or improving processes to reduce cost, leaders are continually asking questions and learning what might be done differently. This is not about changing just for the sake of change. A leader is continually assessing and balancing three competing questions that are important for successful and sustainable organizational change.

> ### ➤ What performance is required now?

> By knowing the industry, competitors, and general market forces, leaders have both a quantitative and intuitive understanding of what performance is needed to be successful. Stakeholders such as customers, investors, bankers, suppliers, competitors, and employees can provide leaders with important information about the level of performance needed to compete successfully. Competitors may be developing new product features, customers may require shorter order-to-delivery time, or employees may need more information on supplier lead times. These are just some of the issues leaders seek out and hunger to learn more about.

> ### ➤ What are your priorities for improving performance?

> Knowing what performance is required in the broader marketplace opens the question of what to change. The information from customers and others may translate into important changes such as shorter production and delivery cycle times, or better customer service to support new products. All these opportunities must be ranked. A clear vision can help you and your employees identify the more critical opportunities. Remember, you cannot change everything at once so setting priorities is important.

> ### ➤ What is the capacity of the people in the organization to change?

> Skill level and knowledge, project experience, and workload are just some of the factors that can help you assess the capacity of an organization to change. People, including you, will be stretched to learn new skills, knowledge, and behaviors with each change you implement. Assessing the scope of new learning required for any change and matching that to the existing capacity of people to learn and succeed is a critical leadership decision.

This is a balancing act with important consequences. If you overstretch people with too many changes all at once so they do not succeed, you will lose leadership credibility. On the other hand, if you do not pursue enough of the most important changes, you may lose the race to change and your competitor's performance will improve faster than yours will.

WHAT IS IMPORTANT FOR YOUR ORGANIZATION?

Think about your own situation and what you know. Read the questions below and write down your initial thoughts. Spend 15 minutes on this. Then talk to other sources of information and ask them these same questions. Write their comments below to begin developing a broader view on these questions.

1. What performance is required of our company in today's market?

My Thoughts:_____

_____

Thoughts of Others:_____

_____

2. What are the company's priorities for improving performance?

My Thoughts:_____

_____

Thoughts of Others:_____

_____

3. What capabilities of our people will be most important in the future, and how are we further developing these today?

My Thoughts:_____

_____

Thoughts of Others:_____

_____

Talking to others about these questions can help guide your change and what you might ask others to change. It is important to listen carefully to what others say and to think how you might contribute to the changes they propose that you had not considered. Have fun with this exploration!

Understanding the Human Response to Change

In today's business world, leaders are constantly asking people to make one change after another. Leaders even have to deal with multiple initiatives that may appear conflicting to some employees. Developing your understanding of how people respond to change is a critical leadership skill that helps employees grow through the change.

Typically, most of us do not like change—particularly when we feel we are not in control or prepared for it. For example, we all like the normal daily routines we develop for ourselves. The routines we develop become second nature to us. Change disrupts these routines, forcing us to stop doing what has become comfortable and familiar to us. We are forced to start learning to do something new and different. This can be upsetting as we enter the zone of the unknown!

A Matter of Choice

Initially, change can be disturbing and difficult. Think of a time when you personally had to change something important to you when you had no real choice. Maybe it was a job that ended unexpectedly or a move to a city you did not know or like. Or maybe it was in childhood when you had to change schools. It could even have been small change such as no longer having your morning coffee at a favorite place. If you had no choice in the change, you probably initially felt disoriented, confused, and even angry. You may have wondered why this was happening to you!

By contrast, when you *choose* to make a change, your reactions are usually very different. For example, if you decide to leave a job for what you believe will be a better position, you will have positive excitement about this change. You will be thinking about the attractive aspects and looking toward the change. You will have thought through this change and will feel you are in control and prepared for whatever may come.

Successful leaders learn how to deal with changes that they initiate as well as changes they cannot control. Leaders take actions that will help prepare the people they are leading for both types of change.

For more information, read *Change Management* by Cynthia Scott and Dennis Jaffe, Thomson Learning.

Recognizing Project vs. Cultural Change

Being a leader requires understanding the many forms that change can take in organizations. This section focuses on two aspects of change: change as part of a project and change as part of a company's culture.

Projects as Change Efforts

Often leaders lead significant organizational change as part of a project. One example of such a project may be the reorganization of multiple, formerly independent centers for customer and technical support into a new global customer and technical support organization working 24/7. As a project, there are clear goals, specific milestones to be met, and challenges to resolve with the expectation of higher performance.

As people drive toward accomplishing the tasks and milestones as part of a project plan, leaders keep their eye on the overall task and the overall process. Delays on key project milestones can cost a project team valuable time and money. But if the process of meeting a milestone violates trust or important relationships, the project may fail and may severely damage future change efforts. Paying attention to what gets done (task) and to how it is being accomplished (process) is very important during change and is a critical leadership responsibility.

Company Culture and Change

Leaders are also concerned about a company's general behavior and attitudes toward making changes. Do people see change as being rewarded and supported by their leadership? Are mistakes seen as learning experiences or opportunities to punish? Going back to the global customer and technical support organization mentioned above, consider the selection of a project manager.

If recent projects have not gone well, it may be difficult to attract the right person to head up the new global center. The company culture may not be seen as supportive of change. Leaders seek to establish conditions in an organization that will allow change to happen as part of how the organization normally operates.

Remember that leaders must use their role, relationship, and knowledge power in times of change while keeping true to the evolving vision for their organization. To help you understand the skills you must develop as a leader, the next few pages will look more closely at what leaders can do for both project and cultural approaches to change.

YOUR ORIENTATION TO CHANGE

Thinking about your own reaction and orientation to change, read the following statements and check (✔) those that reflect your predisposition to change.

❑ I understand that change can be difficult and disruptive to employees.	❑ I do not understand why employees resist change.
❑ I think it is part of my job to help employees through the change.	❑ I become frustrated when employees resist change.
❑ I think allowing employees to try new ways of doing their work is important.	❑ I think employees are less productive when they try new ways of working.
❑ I see mistakes during the change process as important opportunities for learning.	❑ I see mistakes during the change process as something to be avoided.
❑ I believe that team members must trust each other to be successful.	❑ I believe that working on relationship issues is a waste of time.
❑ I believe you can start making changes without having all the answers beforehand.	❑ I believe it is important to know everything that will need to be done to be successful.
❑ I believe people embrace change when they have some say in how change is accomplished.	❑ I believe it is my responsibility to direct all aspects of the change effort.

If you checked more boxes on the left-hand side of the list, you possess an orientation to embracing change and helping your employees successfully navigate through. If you checked more boxes on the right-hand side, you may see change and learning as a problem. Remember that no one ever gets complex organizational change exactly right the first time.

Managing Change Effectively

As your vision takes shape on the job, things will naturally begin to change. To assist you are four major tools in your "change management toolbox":

➤ **Providing rewards**

➤ **Making the new way easier**

➤ **Assuring with optimism**

➤ **Emphasizing learning**

These tools are particularly helpful for projects or other situations where there is a clear goal or change to be achieved. Let's look at how you can put these tools to work to help you effectively manage a specific change.

Providing Rewards

Payoffs or rewards can be extremely effective in bringing about change. Given the change you would like employees to master, what payoffs can you provide when the change occurs? How can you make it rewarding when your employee takes the risk of trying something new? You cannot wait until employees are 100% behind the change or they may never get there. Instead, when you see an employee begin to accept the change, you need to praise and acknowledge the attempt, even if it is not wholehearted or done perfectly. What this means is you are providing a payoff to your employee to make it worth going through this change.

Making the New Way Easier

How can you make the status quo undesirable so that the employee would rather make the change? You may change things so that it takes more time or effort to do it the old way. Or you might remove approval or other social awards that the employee previously received. Often group pressure such as joking or kidding can help some of the most entrenched individuals change old ways.

Assuring with Optimism

Some people are extremely fearful of change. They can see only the downside. As a leader, you must help this person see the benefits of the change. You can do this with reassuring optimism. Consistently state your belief in the worth, impact, and possibility of the change. Do not let the change resisters pull you down with their negativism. If the resister says, "Top management will never support it," the optimistic reply is, "I think once we've presented our ideas, they will be behind us." State what you plan to do to gain the needed support.

Emphasizing Learning

Most change needs practice, feedback, and reflection for important learning to occur. As a leader, you can help accelerate learning by being or providing a coach to an individual or project team. To take the appropriate next step, the following three questions can help people examine their recent experience compared to what was expected:

➤   What just happened?

➤   Why do we think this happened?

➤   What do we need to do about what we have just learned?"

Let's take a look at how these four major change-management tools are applied in the following case study.

CASE STUDY: MANAGING THE WEB SITE PROJECT

Neil, a recent hire and one of the analysts in your department, is responsible for creating your department's pilot intranet. Neil developed skill with a basic Web site software package and was able to put about 15% of your department's most commonly used standard administrative forms, information, and contact data onto the company's intranet in just a few weeks.

The pilot project has proven very successful, and now you want to put more of your department's information and transaction forms onto the site. Bringing up and maintaining the pilot site has taken a large portion of Neil's time and he is justly proud of his initial work. Nearly everyone in the department knows Neil because of the Web site, and he is often acknowledged formally and informally because he did such a good job.

He has balked, however, at doing the much-needed expansion of the site that would complete the project. To finish, Neil would have to coordinate the project and involve others, which would mean he would stop doing all the keystrokes himself.

Recently you have become aware that Neil has missed some milestones associated with revising and expanding the Web site. You are concerned that the pilot may stall without the additional forms and transactions going online. Neil seems to be spending more time maintaining what was developed than working to complete the site. Several of your supervisors have commented to you about Neil's not yet having put their information, forms, and services online.

When you ask Neil about it, he throws up verbal barriers. He says making those changes and maintaining them himself would be impossible. He would need to coordinate with others in the department as well as several vendors. Upgrading and completing the Web site would completely change the current site and his own work.

CONTINUED

You believe Neil has managerial ambitions and potential, but that he may be stuck on doing the Web site project himself. You want to reward Neil for his extraordinary work so far, motivate him to manage this Web site project to completion, and develop Neil's managerial ability in the process.

How would you apply each of the change-management tools to help Neil? Write your responses on the lines provided.

Providing payoffs:_____

_____

_____

_____

Making the new way easier: _____

_____

_____

_____

Assuring with optimism: _____

_____

_____

_____

Emphasizing learning: _____

_____

_____

_____

Compare your answers to the authors' responses in the Appendix.
Your responses do not have to be identical to the authors' but should
convey the same spirit.

Developing a Culture for Change and Learning

Effective leaders know the importance their organization's culture can have on how people approach change. Where attempts to improve performance and learn new methods are supported and encouraged, people know that change is valued. But if change is seen as personally or professionally risky, the current level of performance may be very difficult to improve upon.

Leaders can use the following six practices to create a climate where change and learning become "the usual way we do our work around here."

> **Two-Way Communication:** In their communication, leaders seek to understand how others see a situation so they can become more effective in guiding the right course of action. Using open-ended questions and sincerely listening to others' views are critical skills. People will take more calculated risks when they feel they are both heard and understood.

> **Learning from Experience:** Creating a non-threatening climate where people can learn from their experiences is a valuable practice to develop as a leader. This may be as simple as a routine, quick review of staff meetings or a more extensive project review where learning something new is valued. Think of the impact leaders have if after a "failure" they seek not to assign blame, but instead gather people to develop a deeper understanding of what really happened, thoughts on why this particular result occurred, and what needs to be done differently in the future. This includes how the leaders themselves may have contributed to the "failure." Moving from blame to learning can shift people to be more trusting about taking a risk to improve performance, even if it does not work out perfectly the first time.

> **Shared View:** Leaders share their understanding of what is important with their staff. Talking about the business challenges facing the department and company can help staff members build a shared view of what is going on and what is important. Using real situations or hypothetical ones can help people exercise and strengthen their own thinking and build confidence.

➢ **Seeing the Whole System:** Leaders help employees to see how their contributions fit into the overall company as a system. Some leaders use performance scorecards to provide both quantitative and qualitative information about performance and initiatives. Others use flow diagrams to portray the complex interconnections to be coordinated. In staff meetings, the conversation might shift toward what everyone can do to improve a valued performance metric or result.

➢ **Make Local Changes:** Leaders support small changes and local experiments to improve performance. Sponsoring simple, local experiments to change performance stimulates people to try out new ideas and learn. This helps them build confidence in you and their abilities to make the right decision on important trade-offs.

➢ **Valuing Personal and Professional Development:** Leaders can create the expectation that personal and professional developments are important and valued. When new skills or behaviors are needed to support a change, people will have developed confidence in their ability to learn and experiment with new methods.

Keeping Current with Continuous Learning

As a leader, you must keep your knowledge power current. A serious oversight some managers make is not attending to their personal leadership growth. Just as with employees, what you know and do today will not be sufficient for the rapidly changing business environment.

You cannot let personal growth slide until you "have the time." That time will never come. You must have a development plan for yourself. If you do not write it down, another "crisis" will take priority. Assess your development needs and then take appropriate action. Use the space below to add your own ideas.

Ask yourself if you need to learn more about:

➤ Trends in your company's industry

➤ What your customers and suppliers want and how their world is changing

➤ How your company fits into the overall economy

➤ Your competitors

➤ Leading change

➤ New technology developments

What Do I Need to Know?	How Am I Going to Learn It?	By When?
The latest trends in my industry.	Hear an industry forecaster speaking at an association meeting.	Dec. 20

Fostering Ongoing Improvement in Your Workplace

People normally fall into two groups: those who create their future and those who let others create it. Leaders are solidly in the first group.

Leaders are never satisfied with the status quo. They are always looking for ways to do things better. True leaders seem to overflow with new ideas. These ideas come from constantly scanning the environment for trends and new possibilities. But the focus on improvement is not just products or services—it is also the people.

As a leader, an important message to your staff is that everyone, regardless of experience or job title, should be constantly improving. Daily work becomes an ongoing classroom. Ways to foster personal improvement include:

➤ Attending outside workshops and seminars

➤ Working directly with employees to share insights

➤ Devising group projects for cross training

➤ Reviewing projects with your staff to learn something new

➤ Visiting other organizations or departments

➤ Developing or attending in-house training courses

➤ Encouraging special projects that enhance skills and abilities

➤ Reading books, journals, and articles

One company president holds a monthly book-review meeting with her key managers. The president selects one book a month related to business. All read the book and then discuss which ideas are appropriate for their business.

Whatever avenue you use, the message you send when you encourage growth is that you encourage people to expand their skills and knowledge.

For more information on personal growth, read *Successful Lifelong Learning* by Bob Steinbach, Thomson Learning.

Summary of Part 4

Part 4 on being a change agent has presented the following points for leaders:

- ❑ Great leaders see change as a significant part of their job and are able to help those they are leading to transition from one change right into another.

- ❑ As leaders constantly look for ways to improve performance, they reexamine what new performance is required to remain competitive, setting clear priorities about what needs to change and enhancing the change capabilities of the people in the organization.

- ❑ Change disrupts familiar routines, and people are forced to learn something new and often very different from the past.

- ❑ When change is part of a project, leaders can use the tools of providing rewards, making the change easier, being positive, and emphasizing learning as an act of leadership.

- ❑ When change is part of an organization's culture, leaders will have highly developed skills in two-way communication, learning from experience, developing a shared view with others, seeing and thinking about the whole organization as a system, supporting local change experiments, and valuing personal and professional development.

- ❑ Leaders must be continual learners, hungry for new ideas, information, and challenges.

- ❑ Leaders create a climate and expectation that everyone in the organization should be constantly seeking ways to improve performance.

P A R T 5

Being a Team Leader

68

Bringing People Together into Teams

Teams and teamwork have become important sources for improving performance in organizations. By bringing together people with different talents and perspectives, teams can develop and even experiment with new ideas to improve their performance. This is called synergy. But it is not guaranteed. Leaders learn how to assess and develop teams to achieve new levels of performance.

Teams have both a technical and human dimension. Part of your job as a leader is to bring together the technical skills of your team members. But a larger part of your job as leader is to bring together the people to support one another in overcoming the technical challenges. The human dimension of teams is one of the most difficult aspects of leading a team.

As the leader, you must keep the team focused on what is truly important and what can be accomplished. In this part, you will learn the five critical factors for enabling people to work well together as a team:

> ➤ Working toward common goals

> ➤ Knitting together various responsibilities

> ➤ Developing the human side of teams

> ➤ Resolving conflict productively

> ➤ Increasing trust through trustworthiness

Growing your team and its ability to work together depends on periodic assessment of how well the team is doing. Turn the page for a framework for such an assessment.

Assessing Team Effectiveness

It is one thing for you, the team leader, to assess the team's effectiveness, but leaders often score their teams higher than the team members themselves do. That is why it is helpful to also have your team members provide individual assessments.

The exercise on the following page can be used for this purpose. Simply make copies to give to your team members to complete anonymously. Then collect the completed assessments and summarize the results.

Discussing Your Scores

When you report the results to the team, provide for each question the average score as well as the lowest and highest scores. This allows the team to see not only the overall averages, but also how closely clustered or dispersed the members' views about the team are. Then you can lead a discussion on your team's effectiveness by focusing on the two questions that got the highest scores (strengths) and the lowest scores (weaknesses).

It is important to keep this discussion from being a finger-pointing session. You as the leader must frame the discussion as an opportunity to further grow your team and its ability to work together. As the leader, you must be both accepting and supportive of whatever the scores and responses are. This is an opportunity for you to model how to have an open discussion on group issues. If done well, your acceptance and support will demonstrate your trustworthiness to the team members, who in turn will be more willing to be open and share their ideas, thoughts, information, feelings, and opinions.

If there are two or three areas that could improve the team's effectiveness, limit the number of goals to the critical few. Later, you can assess again and lead the team to selecting the next set of goals to work on. After the exercise, the next section will assess your team's common goals.

How Well Is the Team Working?

Indicate your assessment of the team and the way it functions by circling the number on each scale that you feel is most descriptive of your team.

We don't know the goals, objectives, and priorities.	1 2 3 4 5	Team members understand and agree on goals, objectives, and priorities.
There is little trust among team members and conflict is evident.	1 2 3 4 5	There is a high degree of trust among members, and conflict is dealt with openly and worked through.
One person dominates, and leadership roles are not carried out or shared.	1 2 3 4 5	There is full participation in leadership, and members share leadership roles.
We are guarded and cautious in team discussions.	1 2 3 4 5	We are open and authentic in team discussions.
We do not listen to each other.	1 2 3 4 5	We listen, understand, and are understood.
We operate on the basis of everyone for himself/herself.	1 2 3 4 5	We show genuine concern or for each other.
There is no consistent way problems are solved or decisions are made.	1 2 3 4 5	The team has well-established and agreed-upon approaches to problem solving and decision-making.
The team members are unclear in their roles, responsibilities, and performance expectations.	1 2 3 4 5	There is clarity in team members' job roles and responsibilities.

CONTINUED

========CONTINUED========

Important issues are often   1 2 3 4 5   Important issues are
swept under the carpet and   openly discussed includ-
not worked through.   ing how people feel.

There is little acceptance and 1 2 3 4 5   There is significant ac-
support among the team   ceptance and support
members.   among the team mem-
                                                bers.

Add up your scores to the questionnaire. If your overall score is between 40 and 50, congratulations! You and your team are doing well. If you scored between 20 and 40, your team needs a tune-up. If your overall score was less than 20, your team needs serious attention.

Working Toward Common Goals

Imagine a group of people playing football. But no one has established where the goal line is. It will be almost impossible to win the game, and the players are likely to trip each other up and may even become resentful about the other team members' actions. This is what happens to your team if they do not know and embrace their common goals.

Examining Your Team's Goals

At a department meeting have each of your team members write on a sheet of flip chart paper what they believe to be the top three goals of your team. Then hang these on the wall and look for similarities and disparities.

If the goals are primarily the same, congratulations; you have done a great job! But if some are similar and others are different, now is the time to focus and clarify with your team the most critical goals they hold in common.

If the goals are all over the map, you have some work to do. Devote a meeting to department goal setting. Your team must identify what it contributes to the larger organization and what its most critical goals are. Write these down. Make sure everyone has a copy. And revisit them in future staff meetings and employee discussions.

Checking for Conflicting Goals

Often managers inadvertently create competing goals on their team. If you see team members frequently getting into conflict with each other, look to see if their individual responsibilities are at odds with each other, as in the following example.

The Real Problem Between Xavier and Sheriene

Xavier, the team member in charge of sales, has frequent run-ins with Sheriene, who is responsible for the credit function on the team. Xavier's job is to generate as many sales as possible, regardless of the customer's credit worthiness. Sheriene, on the other hand, is responsible for limiting any loss in accounts receivable from customers not paying their bills.

As a result, Xavier sees Sheriene as a bottleneck limiting his ability to be a successful salesperson, while Sheriene sees Xavier as reckless with some of his sales, being a potential credit risk to the company. They each see each other as the problem when the real problem is Jason, their team leader. Jason has not set a common goal for Xavier and Sheriene and the rest of his team.

Jason's challenge is to develop with his team a common goal that would allow, and even force, Xavier and Sheriene to work together and be successful. The purpose of Jason's sales department is to generate revenue for the company without exceeding an aggregate risk level of four on a five-point scale. That forces Xavier and Sheriene to work together to maximize revenues without exceeding the targeted risk level.

Conflicting goals may not explain all conflict on a team, but they may be a significant source of difficulty.

Who on your team frequently has conflicts with others?

_____

Do team members have competing responsibilities?

_____

What goal might you craft that would create a new shared responsibility?

_____

Knitting Together Varied Responsibilities

Teams often bring together people with different professional skills and disciplines. Sorting out and maintaining how individual responsibilities come together to produce valued results is a critical factor to a team's success.

Of course a leader must understand each of the team member's responsibilities and even go one step beyond. Leaders also must help all employees understand how they support one another to attain their common goals. This is an ongoing activity as individual roles and responsibilities evolve, as illustrated in the following example.

Ineffective Integration of Roles

Marta was hired as an administrative assistant in a government relations department in a large pharmaceutical company. Unlike the other assistants who supported individuals, her primary job was to support a community outreach program. The program leaders told Marta that they desperately needed administrative help and that she was to focus solely on supporting this outreach program. As a result, Marta did not do what the other administrative assistants did, such as answering the phones, keeping schedules, and covering during breaks.

Tension began to build in the department. Lucy, the manager, was mystified about why there seemed to be so much conflict, and she organized a team-building session to sort out what was causing the conflict. During the session, Lucy began to see the source of the problem.

Each of the administrative assistants had complained to the individuals they supported. They said that Marta, and thus by implication the outreach program, thought that she was more important than the rest of the department. At the same time, Marta thought she was simply doing what she had been told to do when she was hired.

It is not unusual for employees to have misperceptions about others' responsibilities as the administrative assistants had about Marta. Often this is the result of a mistake that managers, like Lucy, commonly make. Lucy had an aerial view of her department. She saw all the functions and how they were connected. She assumed the rest of the department knew what she knew, but they did not. As in the example, this lack of communication often results in resentment, resistance, and conflict.

To resolve the conflict, Lucy must call a meeting or team-building session, during which the team members can share their perspective of their jobs and identify the support they need. After discussion, specific agreements can be made on how the group will support each other in doing the work of the department. Regular check-ins during staff meetings could flag major projects and work that will require collaboration within the team.

In the example above, Marta initially had to devote all her energies to the outreach program. But once the program was running smoothly, her work demands began to diminish and she could pitch in to help the other administrative assistants.

Effective leaders use a process by which people learn and understand the purpose and structure of one another's jobs, what kind of support they can expect, and who they are expected to support. Periodic readjustments must be addressed explicitly to avoid flare-ups and damaged relationships from work changes.

Developing the Human Side of Teams

Think of the worst team you have ever been on. It probably was not the task demands or confusions, but the personal relationships among team members that made this experience so miserable.

If you put together a group of people and ask them to work on a problem, *they will have differences*. This is a given. The only question is whether they will deal with and positively manage those differences. As the following example illustrates, a team cannot be effective in meeting its goals if it does not resolve its interpersonal problems.

Improving Technical Performance by Improving Human Performance

In one team over several years, the importance of the human side of teams in improving technical performance began to emerge. In team-building sessions at Acme Corporation, the stated goal was to "get more parts out the door." Employees believed that if only they worked at coordinating their technical activities, they would become more productive.

In the first sessions, some of the roadblocks became obvious. Although the technical issues were raised and discussed, there appeared to be little commitment to coming up with a plan that everyone could support. Much of the time in team-building sessions was spent posturing for the boss and one-upsmanship. Agreements were made in the sessions, but team members seldom followed through on these agreements. This raised resentments. But these were never discussed openly in the team. Instead, team members spent time in the corridors and behind closed doors talking about other members.

What the team did not realize was that until they dealt with the interpersonal issues, they were never going to "get more parts out the door."

Managers often think it is not their right or responsibility to delve into these interpersonal issues. They are afraid this will open a Pandora's box of problems.

Leaders, on the other hand, realize that nothing could be more important to the life of a successful team. Leaders understand that conflict and differences are inevitable on teams; and if dealt with effectively, they can have a huge impact on the team's productivity and satisfaction.

An important first step is analyzing the human side of your team from several dimensions, as outlined in the following series of questions. These will help you discover if you need to give attention to the human side of your team's development.

Yes   **No**

❏   ❏   Do team members become defensive when performance or team issues are raised?

❏   ❏   Do employees come to you to complain about each other, rather than talking to each other directly?

❏   ❏   Do team members try to persuade each other about their "solution" rather than listening to each other?

❏   ❏   Do team members complain to you about problems, expecting that you should fix them on your own?

❏   ❏   When difficult issues are discussed in meetings, do team members avoid a meaningful discussion of the problem?

❏   ❏   Do team members continue to argue, even when they are in agreement?

❏   ❏   Do some team members believe there are hidden agendas on the team?

Answering "yes" to any of these questions is an indicator to spend time developing your team's human side.

Turning Conflict into Team Cohesiveness

Ironically, it is through conflict that teams develop cohesiveness. This may sound counterintuitive, but it is by talking about problems and resolving them effectively that we come to trust others.

As an example, think of your best friend—someone to whom you can say anything. Your friend may not necessarily agree with you but will try to understand the situation from your perspective. It is through this open and honest communication that cohesiveness and trust develop. Conversely, if you have to be cautious about what you say to someone for fear of upsetting the person, you will never feel cohesive with that individual.

The key to transforming conflict into cohesiveness and trust is making the conflict productive. Productive conflict produces these positive results:

- ➤ Problems get dealt with

- ➤ Hidden agendas go away

- ➤ Team members develop a deeper understanding of others' views of the same situation

- ➤ Team members' talents are recognized and better used

- ➤ The team is more likely to achieve and even exceed its common goals

- ➤ Discussions are more honest

- ➤ Team members enjoy being together

Unless your team is competent in dealing with conflict, you will need to explicitly model and teach the team how to have productive conflict. The elements of turning conflict and differences into productive solutions are covered in the next sections.

Setting the Tone for Resolving Conflict Productively

Making conflict productive begins with fundamentally changing the tone of the conflict from attack and defend to a give-and-take discussion about the conflict. The goal is to shift conflict effectively into productive conversations that preserve important interpersonal relationships.

Following the five steps outlined below will ensure the discussion is based on a demonstrated willingness of one party to hear and understand the other.

1. Avoid Defensiveness: When someone else attacks, it is a natural inclination to explain our behavior and defend ourselves because we humans do things for reasons that make sense to us. But defending causes the other person to attack even more. And if we continue to defend, we set up a cycle of attack followed by defense, which does not solve the issue. Defensiveness shuts down communication. For productive conflict, it is critical to keep communication open.

2. Actively Listen: Instead of defending, what you must do is actively listen. This means trying to understand the problem from the other person's perspective. You must get behind their eyeballs and see the issue the way they do. You have to understand the issue the way they see it.

3. Paraphrase: Most people in conflict do not feel that their issue has been heard or understood. One way to prove to others that you have heard and understand their position is to paraphrase back to them what you perceive the problem to be. Then ask them if your summary accurately captures their position. This helps open further communication.

4. Acknowledge the Other Person's Position: After there is agreement that you have heard and understood the other person, it may be appropriate to validate how the other person is feeling, even if you do not agree with the facts as the other person sees them, such as: "You know, if I were in your shoes I'd be angry too." You are not saying the other person is right. What you are saying is, "If the world looked to me as it does to you, I would have similar feelings."

5. Focus on the Future, Not the Past: It is natural in conflict to want to tell the other person in detail how they have created a problem for you. But the past is past and cannot be changed. A better strategy is for both parties to focus on the future.

For more tips on effective listening, read *The Business of Listening* by Diana Bonet, Thomson Learning.

CASE STUDY: EFFECTIVE CONFLICT RESOLUTION

Michelle is sitting at her desk working frantically on a hot project. Stephanie appears at her door blurting, "You said you'd get that information to me by 3:00 today. And when you didn't, I had to go to the meeting without it. Everybody there was irritated with me because I didn't have the information. You left me high and dry!"

Michelle's natural inclination is to explain that she had every intention of getting the information to Stephanie, but that at the last minute, her boss gave her a hot project and she had no option but to direct her energies to that.

Instead, Michelle tries to understand the embarrassment that Stephanie experienced. Michelle asks Stephanie: "So, when you showed up at the meeting without the data, everyone jumped on you?"

Stephanie responds, "You got that right!"

Michelle continues, "You know, if I were in your shoes, I'd be very angry with me as well."

Stephanie persists about the problem, in part because she is concerned that Michelle may not follow through on her requests in the future. So Michelle responds, "I'm so sorry I didn't get you the data on time. My boss gave me a hot project at the last minute, and I didn't have a choice. I left you a voice mail, but it must have been too late. Tell you what—how about if I promise you that if I make a commitment to you in the future, and a conflicting assignment comes up, I will get in touch with you in person within five minutes to figure out what we can do."

From the experience she just went through, Stephanie was concerned that Michelle might let her down again sometime. But with an agreed-upon plan on how work assignment conflicts will be managed in the future, Stephanie is much more likely to let go of her anger toward Michelle and not continue her attack.

Learning to Lead

CONTINUED

Consider Michelle's actions and make note of the points at which she took each step in setting the tone for making her conflict with Stephanie productive. Again, the five steps are:

1. Avoid defensiveness: _____

2. Actively listen: _____

3. Paraphrase: _____

4. Validate: _____

5. Focus on the future: _____

Think of a conflict you have had in the past. What could you have said that would have switched the focus to the future?

_____

_____

_____

See the authors' analysis of the case study in the Appendix.

Describing vs. Evaluating Others' Behavior

You have learned that setting the tone for making conflict productive begins with avoiding defensiveness. Not only should you avoid your own defensiveness, but also you must avoid making the other person defensive. And people are much more likely to become defensive when we *evaluate* their behaviors, as opposed to merely *describing* them. For example, if you say to someone, "You are lazy," you are likely to get a defensive response, such as "No I'm not!"

Defensive responses come in part from feeling unable to fix the "problem" because we do not know what behavior you are focused on. After the comment about laziness, what behavior should the person change to fix it? Come in earlier? Walk faster? Clean her desk? Evaluative comments put people in a box with no way out. Therefore, a defensiveness reaction is likely.

On the other hand, descriptive comments are specific, identifying behaviors that the person might work to change. Descriptive comments, by definition, are based on facts rather than opinions. Thus, the person hearing the description knows exactly what behaviors have caused the conflict with you.

Read the first two evaluative and descriptive comments. Then write your own descriptive comments with specific behaviors for each of the following evaluative comments.

Evaluative Comments	Descriptive Comments
"You have a bad attitude!"	*"When I asked for help yesterday, you told me to go jump in the lake."*
"You are not dependable."	*"I thought we had a 9:00 meeting this morning. I waited in the conference room until 9:20, and you didn't show up."*
"You are incompetent in your job."	_____ _____
"You don't care about the team."	_____ _____
"You never get things done on time."	_____ _____
"Your work is sloppy."	_____ _____

Discerning Content Conflicts vs. Relationship Conflicts

A common reason for an inability to resolve conflict is when one person thinks it is a content conflict while the other person is having a relationship conflict.

A content conflict is based on facts being discussed. For example, two individuals differ on the fastest way to get from point A to point B, so they agree to get into their cars, and the first person to arrive at point B is right. Or two people differ on the definition of a word, so they agree to look it up in a dictionary. These are examples of content conflicts.

A relationship conflict is about behaviors between people. For example, "I think you are trying to sabotage me," "You are trying to make me look like a fool in meetings," or "You are always trying to one-up me in front of the boss." These are examples of relationship conflicts.

Conflict on the Project Team

Matt and Gary are members of an important project team. Gary sees Matt as always trying to draw attention to his contributions and achievements. Gary resents Matt's continuous self-promoting behavior.

Today in the staff meeting, whenever Matt brought up an idea, Gary's response was, "That won't work." Matt would then try to explain the logical rationale behind his idea. Gary continued to dismiss Matt's ideas during the meeting. Matt would then continue to explain his logic, to which Gary would continue to raise reasons that Matt's ideas could not work.

Although it looks like these two individuals are having a conflict, in truth, they have two different conflicts. Gary is having a relationship conflict and Matt is having a content conflict.

In this example, Matt believes his differences with Gary are about content (the workability of his ideas) while Gary is having a relationship conflict with Matt about Matt's self-promoting behavior.

Matt must recognize that his logical and rational answers are not working and ask himself if the conflict has something to do with behavior—and address it if it is. And if Gary could have an honest discussion with Matt about how he sees Matt's behavior as serving himself more than the team, the team would be better served.

HOW DO YOU APPROACH CONFLICTS?

If a problem arises, do you automatically look for a relational issue as the source or a content issue? Take a look at the situations that follow. In each scenario, response A reflects a relational point of view, and response B reflects a content point of view. Which are you more likely to choose?

1. You received some critical feedback from your boss today. She said, "Your work has not been up to par lately." You:

A. Wonder if the comment you made the other day about her son upset her.

B. Take a critical look at your performance to see if her comment has any merit.

2. Scott told you this morning that he hates it when co-workers use all the paper in the copier and don't refill it. You:

A. Wonder if he thinks you are the culprit.

B. Agree that it drives you nuts too.

3. Your boss, who knows you have been having problems at home, informs you that an important client requested that you meet him next week about a major project he wants to give your firm. This means you must be out of town for three days. You:

A. Wonder why he would ask you to do such a thing. After all, he knows about your difficulties at home. You thought he would be more sensitive.

B. Book your flight with the understanding that this client could put your firm on the map.

4. Kristin keeps resisting your recommendation. When you ask what is behind her balkiness, her responses do not make sense to you. You:

A. Wonder if you are doing something to offend her.

B. Take a hard look at the facts and your assessment of the situation.

Whichever choices you made, be careful not to misread a conflict just because you are accustomed to approaching it from a habitual vantage point.

From In the Company of Women, by Pat Heim, Susan Murphy, and Susan Golant. NY: Tarcher/ Putnam, (c) 2001.

Refraining from Conflict in Writing

It is always dangerous to engage in conflict in writing. What starts off as an innocuous comment or request can quickly spiral downward into a batch of ugly exchanges involving an ever-increasing circle of innocent bystanders who have to figure out what is going on and whom to support. The following example illustrates the spiral in action.

Spencer and Jim's Downward Spiral of E-Mail

Spencer is told by his boss at 1:00 P.M. that he must have a report done on the S-51 shipping status by noon tomorrow. The boss says this is a top priority for Spencer. There is an important meeting with the customer and Spencer's boss wants to be prepared. Spencer, feeling the pressure, sends the following e-mail to Jim in the Texas plant.

1:14 P.M. "Jim, I must have the status on all S-51 shipments by the end of the day. Spencer."

Jim's reaction is, "Who does Spencer think he is—my boss?" Jim sends the following e-mail back to Spencer.

1:32 P.M. "Spencer, I'll get you the numbers when I can. Jim."

Spencer thinks he has been put off and put down, and fires back...

2:05 P.M. "Jim, let me be clear. I need the numbers by the end of the day," and Spencer copies his boss on the e-mail.

2:17 P.M. "Spencer, we actually do work in this plant, believe it or not. You'll get your numbers when I can get to them," and Jim copies his boss on this e-mail.

2:22 P.M. "Jim, if I don't get the numbers soon, there may be no more work in your busy plant," and Spencer copies his boss, Jim's boss, the entire team, and a friend in marketing.

2:26 P.M. "Spencer, apparently the gods at corporate are out of touch with what it takes to make the S-51." He copies his boss, Spencer's boss, the plant manager, and all the members of a process improvement team.

Analyzing This Conflict

Does this flurry of e-mails look familiar? The reason conflict in writing can go awry so easily is that the sender of the message receives no cues about the recipient's reaction to the communication. By contrast, if the sender's communication in person or on the phone is misinterpreted by the recipient, the sender gets immediate verbal or non-verbal cues about how the message is being mis-read and can adjust the message quickly before the issue escalates into a full-blown conflict.

In the example, when Spencer got his first clipped response from Jim, he could easily have picked up the phone and said, "Sorry, buddy. I hate to push you on this, but the boss here has given me a tight deadline for this report. When do you think you can get the info to me?"

Conversely, when Jim received what he saw as the first pushy e-mail, he too could have picked up the phone and said to Spencer, "Gosh, we are swamped with shipping orders and doing inventory. Do you really need this information by the end of the day?"

There are few rules that are absolutes about conflict. This, however, is one of them: Never engage in conflict in writing. Even if the other person is in another country, at least pick up the phone and make the call.

Promoting Direct Communication Among Team Members

Few things can erode team cohesiveness and trust as adversely as team members talking negatively to each other about another team member. As a leader, it is your responsibility to ensure this does not happen.

If team members know or suspect that they are being talked about behind their back, you will never have a team that has trust and cohesion. Even subtle comments from you as the leader, such as "Well, you know how Jessica is," can give the impression that it is okay to talk negatively about team members.

So what can you do to prevent this destructive dynamic? State explicitly to employees individually and as a team that you expect them to deal directly with each other when they have a problem. Explain that this is critical for team cohesiveness and trust.

If an employee complains to you about another team member, your response should be, "Have you talked to him about this problem? If you haven't, then don't tell me. I expect that each of us will first talk directly to the person with whom we are having a difficulty."

If you hear that one team member has been talking negatively about another, confront the person and again state your expectation about direct communication with individuals.

Increasing Trust Within the Team

Effective teams have a climate of honesty and frankness among their team members. People feel they can be open and share ideas, information, thoughts, feelings, and opinions for achieving the team's common goals. It is through this exchange of differing views that new approaches and perspectives emerge. In high-trust teams, all views expressed are received with acceptance and support.

The trust level among team members depends on the *relationships* between people, not their personalities. Although some people may be predisposed to trusting or mistrusting others, it is the quality of a particular relationship, not the personalities, that will define whether the relationship itself is based on trust, or a lack of trust.

Trustworthiness Promotes Trust

The key to building and maintaining trust is being trustworthy. Although trust involves behaviors of openness and sharing, *trustworthiness* behaviors involve acceptance and support.

The more accepting and supportive you are of others, the more likely they will be to disclose to you their own personal thoughts, ideas, theories, conclusions, feelings, and reactions. The more accepting and supportive you are in response to such disclosures, the deeper and more truthful will be the thoughts that another person will share with you. To increase trust on a team, increase the trustworthiness behaviors among the members.

How trusting and trustworthy are you? Complete the self assessment on the next page to find out.

Trust Behaviors

Yes	No	
❏	❏	I freely provide information, opinions, ideas and assistance to others.
❏	❏	I volunteer my time to others who may need help.
❏	❏	I will risk raising a difficult issue in our team.
❏	❏	I speak my mind even if the whole team holds a very different position.
❏	❏	I will provide my views on issues, even if others on the team have more expertise and knowledge.

Trustworthy Behaviors

Yes	No	
❏	❏	I listen to the views of others on the team without being critical or evaluating whether they are right or wrong.
❏	❏	I seek opportunities to collaborate with others.
❏	❏	I encourage others to raise important issues on the team that they feel strongly about.
❏	❏	I assist others on the team as they struggle to express their views and paraphrase what they say.
❏	❏	I express my interest to cooperate with others and that they will collaborate and cooperate in response.

Remember, trust exists in relationships, not in the individuals' personalities.

For more information, read *Building Trust* by Mary Shurtleff, Thomson Learning.

Summary of Part 5

Part 5 presents the following points for how to assess and develop teams to achieve new levels of performance.

- It is the leader's responsibility to manage team dynamics.
- Teams must have common goals.
- Leaders must ensure that team members do not have competing goals.
- Teams have more difficulties dealing with their human side than their technical issues.
- Team cohesion comes through productive conflict.
- Making conflict productive begins with setting a positive tone.
- Describing behaviors, rather than evaluating, helps team members see how to resolve a conflict.
- Leaders must distinguish between content and relationship conflicts and make sure their team is addressing the appropriate one.
- Never engaging in conflict in writing or speaking ill of another team member are two absolutes for keeping conflict in check.
- Trust within the team grows from trustworthiness behaviors.

Creating an

Action Plan

94

Ranking Management and Leadership Practices

This survey describes 20 practices that are commonly demonstrated by excellent managers and 20 commonly demonstrated by effective leaders. Please read all statements carefully. Then decide as a manager and leader the priority you would assign each practice or characteristic. Indicate your decision by circling the appropriate number.

	Priority				
	Highest	**High**	**Important**	**Modest**	**Low**
1. Gets tough when needed	5	4	3	2	1
2. Uses knowledge or relationship power over role power	5	4	3	2	1
3. Establishes consistent, clear discipline line	5	4	3	2	1
4. Focuses on the big picture and longer-term future	5	4	3	2	1
5. Provides environment conducive to cohesiveness	5	4	3	2	1
6. Sees change as a learning process	5	4	3	2	1
7. Has full backing of subordinates	5	4	3	2	1
8. Engages employees in creating a vision	5	4	3	2	1
9. Strives to win by allowing employees also to win	5	4	3	2	1
10. Ensures team has common goals	5	4	3	2	1
11. Provides important rewards to staff	5	4	3	2	1
12. Consistently builds up chip surplus	5	4	3	2	1
13. Shows compassion	5	4	3	2	1
14. Values differences and productive conflict	5	4	3	2	1
15. Is a good listener	5	4	3	2	1

CONTINUED

	Priority				
	Highest	**High**	**Important**	**Modest**	**Low**
16. Understands organization's priorities	5	4	3	2	1
17. Expresses thoughts clearly	5	4	3	2	1
18. Integrates responsibilities of the team	5	4	3	2	1
19. Keeps employees fully informed	5	4	3	2	1
20. Is able to deal with the human side of the team	5	4	3	2	1
21. Is highly ethical	5	4	3	2	1
22. Avoids defensiveness	5	4	3	2	1
23. Delegates effectively	5	4	3	2	1
24. Encourages employees to talk about differences	5	4	3	2	1
25. Shares large and small victories with staff	5	4	3	2	1
26. Does not rely only on role power	5	4	3	2	1
27. Makes work enjoyable	5	4	3	2	1
28. Avoids creating chip deficits	5	4	3	2	1
29. Maintains positive, upbeat attitude	5	4	3	2	1
30. Sees the long view and delegates the details	5	4	3	2	1
31. Admits to mistakes	5	4	3	2	1
32. Understands the difference between relationship conflicts	5	4	3	2	1
33. Follows logical steps in making decisions	5	4	3	2	1
34. Uses non-verbal cues effectively	5	4	3	2	1
35. Consults with others in making decisions	5	4	3	2	1

	Priority				
	Highest	**High**	**Important**	**Modest**	**Low**
36. Relentlessly pursues improved performance	5	4	3	2	1
37. Uses management role with sensitivity	5	4	3	2	1
38. Is trustworthy	5	4	3	2	1
39. Is respected by employees when authority is used	5	4	3	2	1
40. Avoids engaging in conflict in writing	5	4	3	2	1

All of the above practices found in effective managers have odd numbers. Those practices not always found in managers but usually found in leaders have even numbers.

Please add up all the numbers circled in the *odd-numbered* statements and enter into this box:

Management
Practices

Please add up all the numbers circled in the *even-numbered* statements and enter into this box:

Leadership
Practices

Interpreting Your Scores

1. Scoring higher in this Management and Leadership Practices survey than on the Personal Management Assessment Scale in Part 1 indicates that becoming more familiar with leadership practices has improved your managerial awareness. This is very positive. You may also consider developing your leadership skills by selecting a few areas and goals in the next few pages. But remember that your first priority should be on your managerial abilities.

2. If your score in the Leadership Practices box is 80 or more, it would appear you are ready to take on more of a leadership role. In the next few pages you will be setting goals to solidify your leadership skills.

3. A Leadership Practices score between 60 and 80 may indicate that you are getting ready to move into a leadership role. Your goals may require more time to execute, so be patient and work on the fundamental areas to improve your leadership performance.

4. A Leadership Practices score substantially less than your Management Practices score may indicate that leadership, at this time, may not be for you. You may want to reexamine your interest in leadership to see if it is truly what you want. It may be that if you can find a purpose that excites you, your interest in developing your leadership abilities will increase. Remember, the best leaders are passionate about making a difference.

5. Please list any additional interpretations that you make from the results of your assessments.

_____

_____

_____

_____

_____

_____

Identifying Skills to Be Strengthened

If you have chosen to develop your leadership skills, you probably have a number of specific skills you think are important to strengthen. As has been discussed in this book, it is often easy to get caught up in daily crises and lose sight of long-term objectives.

Take a few minutes now to plan for your own leadership development. What area(s) would you like to focus on developing in the next few months?

- ❑ Using knowledge power
- ❑ Using relationship power
- ❑ Creating chip surpluses
- ❑ Using non-verbal communication more effectively
- ❑ Maintaining a positive attitude
- ❑ Creating vision with employees
- ❑ Seeing the organization's big picture
- ❑ Delegating the details
- ❑ Communicating your vision
- ❑ Working with stakeholders
- ❑ Setting specific goals
- ❑ Seeing change as learning
- ❑ Learning about a new technology or method
- ❑ Preparing employees for change
- ❑ Setting common team goals
- ❑ Integrating team responsibilities
- ❑ Making conflict productive
- ❑ Addressing team conflicts and differences
- ❑ Developing trustworthiness

Setting Goals for Leadership Development

True leaders are constantly developing their abilities. On the previous page, you identified leadership skills you would like to develop. Select three to five of these to work on over the next three to six months and list them below. Then use the lines under each skill you list to write the leadership development goals that will help you develop that skill. Remember, goals must be specific, measurable, reasonable, and time-specific.

1. _____

_____

_____

2. _____

_____

_____

3. _____

_____

_____

4. _____

_____

_____

5. _____

_____

_____

Communicating Your Development Plan

You are much more likely to stay on track and achieve your development plan if you share your plan and intentions. Identify below two or three individuals with whom you will discuss your plan to gain their support and feedback on your goals. These may include your current manager, leaders you admire, or other individuals who possess and exhibit the skills you are trying to develop.

Individual: | **How frequently will you check in with this person?** | **Outcomes you desire:**

_____   _____   _____

_____   _____   _____

_____   _____   _____

_____   _____   _____

_____   _____   _____

Drafting Your Leadership Self-Portrait in Six Months

The final step is to create a description of your desired leadership self-portrait six months from now. What qualities, skills, and accomplishments will you have attained in six months as you achieve the goals you have set for yourself?

Write a couple of paragraphs as you expect others would describe you and your leadership abilities six months from now. Be specific about how you would like others to see you and your leadership behavior.

_____

_____

_____

_____

_____

_____

_____

_____

_____

_____

_____

_____

_____

_____

_____

_____

_____

_____

_____

A P P E N D I X

Authors' Suggested Responses to Case Studies

Selecting the Best Available Model (Page 29)

Crystal made a smart move in switching role models. Some organizations develop many good managers but few leaders. In these firms, managers usually stay in their present positions longer. In almost all organizations, leadership is the key to greater upward mobility.

Expanding Your Vision (Page 35)

Managers focus primarily on their unit's performance, while leaders focus on the organization's overall results and performance. If Donny had built his knowledge power he would know that the company was having a significant scrap problem of $6 million a year. This was eroding the company's bottom-line performance, and valued customers were upset. With this knowledge Donny might have approached Fred differently to work out the problem in the assembly line. And if Donny had built up relationship power with Fred, solving the technical problem would have been much easier. If Donny were a visionary leader, he would have seen the problem was not Fred, but the scrap rate, and would have joined Fred in solving this important company problem.

Too Much Attention to Detail? (Page 38)

Barbara's dilemma is far more common than she realizes. Employees who receive many accolades for meticulously taking care of details are often rewarded by promotion into management. What they are not told is that their job has fundamentally changed. Their focus must be on vision and long-term goals. Barbara needs the time to see the patterns and trends in her department, organization, and industry.

If you find yourself overwhelmed with details, it is time to look around and figure out to whom to delegate. If you are not sure if it is appropriate to delegate to an employee, consider this approach: "If we can both do it, you do it." Delegating means letting go of responsibilities that others can fulfill.

Pressure from Above (Page 47)

Miranda needs to define and communicate a consistent vision for her department. As new or changing priorities develop, Miranda must help her staff understand how these priorities are consistent with the department's overall vision. For example, if Miranda's vision is outstanding and consistent customer service, then an emphasis on keeping within budget does not mean forsaking quality customer service. Miranda must learn how to incorporate the direction from senior management into her department's vision, goals, and day-to-day priorities. She must eliminate the mixed signals to her staff.

If she does not do this, her staff will remain frustrated and critical of her leadership and the lack of clear priorities. Miranda must give her employees one clear, understandable direction even as the day-to-day activities required from the department may shift. Although change is inevitable, leaders help their employees make sense of shifting priorities and trade-offs without losing sight of the overall vision and goals.

Managing the Web Site Project (Pages 60-61)

Providing Payoffs

a) Discuss with Neil his career opportunities and how completing the Web site through others could help him develop his skills toward becoming an effective manager.

b) Offer him the opportunity to attend a seminar on project management or managing intranet Web sites using the newest programming tools.

c) Praise Neil when he talks to other department heads, other functions in the department, and vendors about their needs for the department Web site.

d) Mention positive feedback you have heard about his attempts to involve others to scope the upgrade project.

e) Identify Web sites he admires from other departments and have him visit those departments to research the techniques they are using and their results.

Making the New Way Easier

a) Stop commenting on the current Web site.

b) Create performance goals for Neil related to his managerial skills in improving and completing the Web site.

c) Give him an assignment that would more easily or professionally be done that involved coordination with others.

d) Limit the amount of time Neil can spend on the Web site project, such as telling him to stop maintaining the site and focus on expanding and completing it.

e) Introduce others in the organization to Web site publishing so they can develop skills needed to support completing and maintaining your department's site.

f) Create a department goal and team with Neil to complete the Web site by a specific date.

Assuring with Optimism

State your beliefs about:

a) The professional, new look the completed Web site will provide the department.

b) Neil's ability to transition from analyst and Webmaster to manager and coordinator.

c) The support you have heard from top management for building the company's intranet.

Emphasize Learning

a) Have Neil meet with other department heads and project managers to hear how they coordinated and completed their department's intranet sites.

b) Have Neil meet with others in the department to discuss how they might organize, complete, and maintain the department's Web site.

c) Ensure Neil knows how the completed Web site fits into your vision for the department.

d) Listen for opportunities to coach Neil in becoming an effective coordinator of others and provide time and praise as he progresses.

e) Talk to Neil about the new skills he would develop from completing this project and what support you might provide him.

(In general, when Neil comments on why it will not work, you state your belief about how it will work.)

Effective Conflict Resolution (Pages 81-82)

1. **Avoid defensiveness**–Michelle doesn't try to explain away the problem.

2. **Actively listen**–Michelle listens and tries to understand Stephanie's embarrassment.

3. **Paraphrase**–Michelle asks Stephanie: "So, when you showed up at the meeting without the data, everyone jumped on you?"

4. **Validate**–Michelle tells Stephanie: "You know, if I were in your shoes, I'd be very angry with me as well."

5. **Focus on the future**–Michelle promises Stephanie that if she makes a commitment to her in the future, and a conflicting assignment comes up, she will get in touch in person within five minutes to figure out what we can do.

Recommended Reading

Bonet, Diana. *The Business of Listening, Third Edition*. Boston, MA: Thomson Learning, 2001.

Chapman, Elwood N. and Wil McKnight. *Attitude: Your Most Priceless Possession, Fourth Edition*. Boston, MA: Thomson Learning, 2002.

Conlow, Rick. *Excellence in Management, Revised Edition*. Boston, MA: Thomson Learning, 2000.

Finch, Lloyd and Robert B. Maddux. *Delegation Skills for Leaders, Third Edition*. Boston, MA: Thomson Learning, 2006.

Fisher, Roger, et al. *Getting to Yes: Negotiating Agreement Without Giving In*. NY: Penguin, 1991.

Harshman, Carl L. and Steven L. Phillips. *Teaming Up: Achieving Organizational Transformation*. San Diego: Pfeiffer and Company, 1994.

Haynes, Marion E. *Time Mangement, Third Edition*. Boston, MA: Thomson Learning, 2001.

Heim, Pat, Susan Murphy, and Susan Golant. *In the Company of Women*. NY: Tarcher/Putnam, 2001.

Holman, Peggy and Tom Devane (eds.). *The Change Handbook: Group Methods for Shaping the Future*. San Francisco: Berrett-Koehler, 1999.

Kouzes, James, et al. *The Leadership Challenge: How to Keep Getting Extraordinary Things Done in Organizations*. San Francisco: Jossey-Bass, 1996.

Mink, Oscar G., et al. *Developing High-Performance People: The Art of Coaching*. Cambridge, MA: Perseus Books, 1993.

Rouillard, Larrie A. *Goals and Goal Setting, Third Edition*. Boston, MA: Thomson Learning, 2003.

Scott, Cynthia and Dennis Jaffe. *Change Management, Third Edition*. Boston, MA: Thomson Learning, 2004.

Scott, Cynthia, Dennis Jaffe, and Glenn Tobe. *Organizational Vision, Values, and Mission*. Boston, MA: Thomson Learning, 1993.

Shurtleff, Mary Galbreath. *Building Trust*. Boston, MA: Thomson Learning, 1998.

Steinbach, Robert. *Successful Lifelong Learning, Revised Edition*. Boston, MA: Thomson Learning, 2000.

Stone, Douglas, et al. *Difficult Conversations: How to Discuss What Matters Most.* NY: Viking, 1999.

Useem, Michael. *The Leadership Moment: Nine True Stories of Triumph and Disaster and Their Lessons for Us All.* NY: Times Business, 1998.

Now Available From

Books•Videos•CD-ROMs•Computer-Based Training Products

Subject Areas Include:

Management

Human Resources

Communication Skills

Personal Development

Sales/Marketing

Finance

Coaching and Mentoring

Customer Service/Quality

Small Business and Entrepreneurship

Training

Life Planning

Writing

VERN